all new
Homespun
Handknit

25 Small Projects to Knit with Handspun Yarn

AMY CLARKE MOORE

INTERWEAVE
interweavestore.com

Photography, Joe Coca
Photo styling + illustration,
Ann Sabin Swanson
Art direction + design, Connie Poole
Production, Katherine Jackson
Technical Editors,
Therese Chynoweth,
Lori Gayle, Carol
Huebscher Rhoades
Copy editor, Katie Banks
Editor, Anne Merrow

Interweave Press LLC
201 East Fourth Street
Loveland, CO 80537-5655
USA
interweavestore.com

Printed in China by Asia Pacific Offset.

Acknowledgments

Thank you, Linda Ligon, for starting Interweave and continuing to contribute your creative genius to numerous projects. Thank you, Marilyn Murphy, for bringing me into the fold of Interweave and nurturing me along the way. Thank you to my family and friends for unquestioning love as well as support and enthusiasm for these projects that I take on—Kelly, Hannah, Mark, Pat, Julia, Ben, Jane, Carol, Sam, Eric, Evan, William, Kevin, Shelly, Briahnna, Brendon, Liz, Vicki, and Judy.

Library of Congress Cataloging-in-Publication Data

Clarke, Amy C., 1969-
 All new homespun handknit : 25 small projects to knit with handspun yarn / Amy Clarke Moore.
   p. cm.
 Includes bibliographical references and index.
 ISBN 978-1-59668-144-6
 1. Knitting—Patterns. I. Title.
 TT825.C53 2009
 746.43'2041--dc22

                         2009010458

10 9 8 7 6 5 4 3 2 1

contents

spinning for knitting

SPINNING AND KNITTING ANEW

Over twenty years ago, I sat on the floor of my dorm room paging through a new book my Aunt Debby had sent me that was full of small handspun and knitted items. I was intrigued—it captured everything that I wanted from a knitting book. I had never considered handspun yarn before, but I loved that the book was a compilation of many people's work and that it gave me the information I needed to head in the right direction. Soon I was churning out socks, and my friends were dropping hints about colors and size. The book was *Homespun, Handknit*, edited by Linda Ligon.

I look back at that moment with wonder at the way things work, the paths we take. I remember looking at the publisher's information and thinking, "What is in Loveland, Colorado?" Little did I know that Loveland was my future—ten circuitous years later I started working at Interweave.

Twenty-two years have passed since I first held *Homespun, Handknit* in my hands. Compiling the next generation of *Homespun, Handknit* is a tall order—but I knew who to call on to fill the pages. Having been the editor of *Spin·Off* since the spring of 2000, I have worked with so

4

many wonderful, talented designers. We live in a great age for handspinning and knitting.

Matching and Substituting Yarn

You don't have to be a handspinner to use this book—all the information you need for substituting yarn, whether handspun or millspun, is provided. If you've only worked with millspun yarns before and feel like your knitting is lacking that certain something, it's probably time to start knitting with handspun. We're riding waves of handpainted, specially blended fibery lusciousness that knitters a few generations ago never dreamed of.

The designers of each project have shared details about the handspun yarns they created—fiber, spinning method, and other measurements—but this book assumes that you go your own way and adapt the pattern to your own needs. Making or finding an exact replica of a yarn is a challenging process, and by necessity as well as design, your rendition of these patterns will be as individual as your yarns. After all, you are unique—shouldn't your knitting be?

Measuring yarn

Most spinners spin yarn and use it without measuring it—and there is nothing wrong with that. But you may one day find yourself needing to describe your yarn to someone else or wanting to match a yarn. It is handy to know the grist (the size of the yarn—usually length per unit weight) of the yarn.

Wraps Per Inch For a quick reference, wrap your yarn around a ruler and count how many wraps fit in one inch to get your wraps per inch. You'll quickly note that the way you wrap your yarn will give you different measurements: you'll get fewer wraps per inch if there are spaces between the yarns, more if they are tightly smooshed together. Wraps per inch is not an exact science. Most people suggest packing the yarn closely, but not overlapping. Don't pull the yarn too tightly while winding it on. If you're consistent with your yarn wrapping, you'll be able to use wraps per inch as a good starting point for figuring out the grist of your yarn.

Yards Per Pound Wraps per inch is a good place to start, but it won't tell you everything you need to know about your yarn. Yards per pound will give you a better idea of how much yarn you need to make for a given project or how much fiber you need to start with to spin yarn for a particular pattern. You can measure your yards per pound by weighing your yarn and counting the yards after you've skeined it on a niddy-noddy, or you can measure a length of yarn on a McMorran balance. (Actually, it is a good idea to do both.)

You can figure yards per pound (ypp) if you know how many yards and ounces are in a skein. You'll have to do a little calculating—there's one useful little trick I retained from math classes.

$$\frac{220 \text{ yds}}{2 \text{ oz}} = \frac{X \text{ yds}}{16 \text{ oz}}$$

If your yarn contains 220 yards and weighs 2 ounces and you want to know the yards per pound (16 ounces), multiply 220 x 16 (which equals 3,520) and divide by 2 to get 1,760 yards.

McMorran Balance

If you have a McMorran balance, all you need is a strand of the yarn to determine the ypp. Place the arm of the balance in the groove at the top of the box with the notched end facing you and hanging over the edge of a table. Place a length of yarn in the notch heavy enough that it makes the arm hang down. With sharp scissors, cut little bits of the yarn off the end (I usually place a wastebasket underneath to catch the cut ends) until the arm balances evenly. When the arm is balanced, take the (now shorter) length of yarn off and measure it. Multiply the inches by 100 and you have yards per pound! A yarn that measures 17½ inches has 1,750 yards per pound.

fair argyle cap

{Erda Kappeler}

This cheerful cap has the look of complicated colorwork but uses only two yarns, one solid and one space-dyed. Erda Kappeler washed Merino/Corriedale fleece by hand and spun the yarn woolen, then fulled the yarn slightly. She dyed one skein a strong blue and painted the other to self-stripe. The fresh, modern yarn is paired with an argyle motif from a Jacquard weaving pattern to create this bold take on a classic.

Spinning Notes

Fiber: 2 oz (57 g) of Merino/Corriedale fleece.
Preparation: Handcarded rolags.
Drafting method: Long draw.
Wheel system: Double drive.
Ratio (singles/plying): 13:1.
Singles direction spun: Z.
Number of plies: 2.
Plied direction spun: S.
Plied twists per inch: 6.
Plied wraps per inch: 12.
Total yardage: 130 yd (119 m).
Yards per pound: 1,040.

Knitting Notes

Yarn classification: Worsted weight (Medium #4).
Yardage used: 98 yd (90 m).
Needles: U.S. size 5 (3.75 mm): set of 5 double-pointed (dpn). Adjust needle size if necessary to obtain the correct gauge.
Gauge: 12 sts and 16 rows = 2" (5 cm).
Finished size: 7½" (19 cm) from brim to top of hat; 20" (51 cm) circumference. To fit a woman's size small.
Note: While working the two-color pattern, carry the inactive yarn loosely in the back and twist it around the working yarn every 4 sts to secure the floats and prevent puckering.

7

CAP

With space-dyed yarn, CO 112 sts. Arrange sts evenly over 4 dpns. Join for working in the rnd, being careful not to twist sts.

RNDS 1–5: *K1, p1; rep from * to end.

Argyle

Work Rnds 1–14 of Argyle chart two times, then work Rnd 1 once.
With blue, knit 1 rnd.

Shape crown

RNDS 1–4: With space-dyed yarn, knit.
RND 5: With blue, *k2tog, ssk, k10; rep from * to end—96 sts rem.
RNDS 6–7: Knit.
RND 8: *K2tog, ssk, k8; rep from * to end—80 sts.
RNDS 9–10: Knit.
RND 11–19: Continue as established, working 2 fewer decreases on each dec rnd—32 sts rem after Rnd 19.
RND 20: *K2tog, ssk; rep from * to end—16 sts rem.
RND 21: Rep Rnd 20—8 sts rem.

Cut yarn, draw through rem sts, and pull tight. Secure tail on WS. Weave in ends.

FINISHING

Roll the cap in a towel, being careful not to wrinkle the cap, and place both in a plastic bag. Wet the towel and cap well and leave to soak for several hours. Remove the cap from the bag and towel and lay it flat to dry on a dry towel.

Argyle

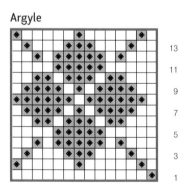

13
11
9
7
5
3
1

Key

☐ eggshell blue (MC)

◈ multi space-dyed (CC)

FAIR ARGYLE CAP

coin purse
{Kathryn Alexander}

This little coin purse started with a handful of pressed pennies. To Kathryn Alexander, they cried out for a quick project that could be finished in a weekend. She designed this bag with two of her signature elements, colorful yarns and modular construction with lots of triangles. Wensleydale top is perfect for a little coin purse: like coins, it is shiny and durable. Kathryn enjoyed spinning the top with a true worsted draw—pulling the fibers down in short increments and keeping the fingers of her forward hand closed—for the challenge of making smooth yarn from the long, hairy top.

Spinning Notes

Fiber: 6 oz (170 g) Wensleydale top, hand-dyed in 12 solid colors and one space-dyed color.

Drafting method: Short draw.

Yarn classification: Worsted.

Wheel system: Double drive.

Ratio (singles/plying): 12:1.

Singles direction spun: Z.

Singles twists per inch: 12.

Singles wraps per inch: 18.

Twist angle: 27°.

Number of plies: 2.

Plied direction spun: S.

Plied twists per inch: 7.

Plied wraps per inch: 12.

Total yardage: 336 (307 m) (25 yd [23 m] each of 12 solid colors and 36 yd [33 m] of space-dyed yarn).

Yards per pound: 896.

Knitting Notes

Yarn classification: Sportweight (Light #2).

Yardage used: About 14 yd (13 m) of each solid color and 36 yd (33 m) space-dyed yarn.

Needles: U.S. size 2 (2.75 mm): two sets of 5 double-pointed (dpn). Adjust needle size if necessary to obtain the correct gauge. *Note:* Bamboo needles are recommended for working with this slippery yarn.

Gauge: 7 sts and 9 rows = 1" (2.5 cm).

Notions: Pennies, buttons, or beads (12 flattened pennies shown); one ⅝" (1.6 cm) shank button; one ¾" (2 cm) shank button; stitch holders; tapestry needle; one piece of fabric about 8" x 16" (20.5 x 40.5 cm) for lining; matching sewing thread and sewing needle.

Finished size: 5¼" (13.5 cm) wide and 5¾" (14.5 cm) long after fulling (not including I-cord fringe).

Yarn Colors

A: Orange
B: Gold
C: Space-dyed
D: Turquoise
E: Emerald
F: Purple
G: Olive
H: Rust
I: Magenta
J: Evergreen
K: Chartreuse
L: Rose
M: Brass

11

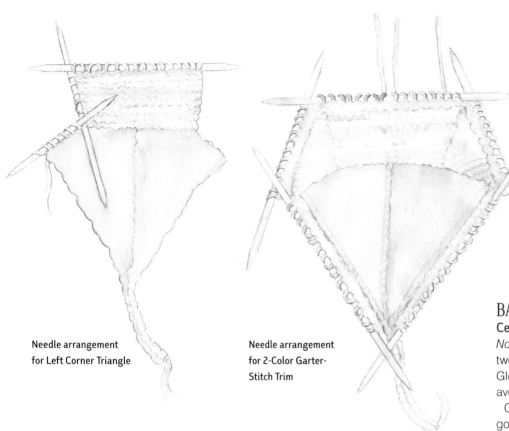

Needle arrangement
for Left Corner Triangle

Needle arrangement
for 2-Color Garter-
Stitch Trim

stitch guide Two-Color 3-Stitch I-Cord

Stitches are always worked using their matching color to create a
vertically striped cord. *With RS facing, k2 with first color, hold first color
strand straight out to the right of the work, and bring the second color
underneath and up in front of the first color, then drop the first color to
the back of the work. K1 with the second color, and with RS facing, slide
the sts back to the beg of the dpn in position to work another RS row. Hold
second color strand straight out to the right of the work, and bring the first
color underneath and up in front of the second color, then drop the second
color to the back of the work.* Rep from * to * for desired length. Pull each
stitch firmly as you work to keep the stitches uniform.

BACK

Center Triangle

Note: Triangle is worked half-and-half in
two colors using the intarsia method (see
Glossary); twist the yarns at the center to
avoid leaving a hole.

CO 16 sts with orange (A) and 16 sts with
gold (B) onto a dpn so that orange (A) sts
will be worked first—32 sts total.

SET-UP ROW: (WS) With A, k16; with B, k16.

ROW 1: (RS) With B, k1, p1, k14; with A,
k14, p1, k1.

ROW 2: With A, k1, p1, purl to color join in
center; with B, purl to last 2 sts, p1, k1.

ROW 3: With B, k1, p1, ssk, knit to center;
with A, knit to last 4 sts, k2tog, p1, k1—2
sts dec'd.

ROWS 4–28: Rep Rows 2 and 3 twelve
more times, then work Row 2 once more
to end with a WS row—6 sts rem, 3 sts
each color.

ROW 29: (RS) With B, k1, p1, ssk (1 st each
of B and A tog); with A, p1, k1—5 sts rem,
3 sts B, 2 sts A.

ROW 30: With A, k1, p1; with B, p2, k1.

ROW 31: With B, k1, sssk (see Glossary; 2
sts B and 1 st A tog); with A, k1—3 sts
rem, 2 sts B, 1 st A.

Work two-color 3-st I-cord (see Stitch Guide) for 5" (12.5 cm). Cut yarns, leaving long tails. Use the tails to attach pennies, buttons, or beads. Knot the ends securely and weave them back into the center of the I-cord.

Garter Panel

With RS facing, hold center triangle pointing down. With space-dyed yarn (C) and RS facing, beg 8 sts before center join, pick up and knit 8 sts along CO edge of triangle to center join, then pick up and knit 8 more sts along CO edge after join—16 sts. Knit 15 rows, beg and ending with a WS row—8 garter ridges completed. Break yarn and place sts on hold.

Right Corner Triangle

With turquoise (D) and RS facing and beg at selvedge of center triangle, pick up and knit 6 sts along CO edge of triangle to beg of garter panel, then 1 st in corner—7 sts. With RS facing, slip a separate dpn into the edge loops of 7 of the 8 garter ridges along selvedge of garter panel; these loops are just placed on the needle, not picked up and knit—14 sts total, 7 sts each on Needles 1 and 2; working yarn is in the middle, between the needles and at the end of Needle 1. Work short-rows as foll:

SHORT-ROW 1: (RS) Sl first st of Needle 1 to Needle 2, ssk (1 st from each needle tog), turn—13 sts, 7 sts on Needle 1, 6 sts on Needle 2.

SHORT-ROW 2: Sl 1 as if to purl with yarn in front (pwise wyf), p1, turn.

SHORT-ROW 3: Sl 1 pwise with yarn in back (wyb), k2, turn.

SHORT-ROW 4: Sl 1 pwise wyf, p3, turn.

SHORT-ROWS 5–13: Continue in St st in this manner, working 1 more st before turning on each row; Row 13 should be worked as sl 1, k12. Break yarn and place sts on hold.

Left Corner Triangle

With RS facing, slip a dpn (Needle 2) into the edge loop of 7 garter ridges along rem selvedge of garter panel as for right corner triangle. With emerald (E) and WS facing and using a separate dpn (Needle 1), pick up and purl (see Glossary) 6 sts along CO edge of center triangle to corner, then 1 st in corner—14 sts total, 7 sts each on Needles 1 and 2; working yarn is in the middle, between the needles and at the end of Needle 1. Work short-rows as foll:

SHORT-ROW 1: (WS) Sl first st of Needle 1 to Needle 2, p2tog (1 st from each needle tog), turn—13 sts, 7 sts on Needle 1, 6 sts on Needle 2.

SHORT-ROW 2: Sl 1 pwise wyb, k1, turn.

SHORT-ROW 3: Sl 1 pwise wyf, p2, turn.

SHORT-ROW 4: Sl 1 pwise wyb, k3, turn.

SHORT-ROWS 5–13: Continue in St st in this manner, working 1 more st before turning on each row; Row 13 should be worked as sl 1, p12. Break yarn and place sts on hold.

2-Color Garter-Stitch Trim

With RS facing and purple (F), beg at I-cord at bottom point of center triangle, pick up and knit 17 sts along selvedge to held right corner triangle sts; with a second dpn and F, knit across 13 sts from holder; with a third dpn and F, pick up and knit 8 sts across BO edge of garter panel to center, then with the same needle and D, pick up and knit 8 sts to end of garter panel BO edge; with a fourth dpn

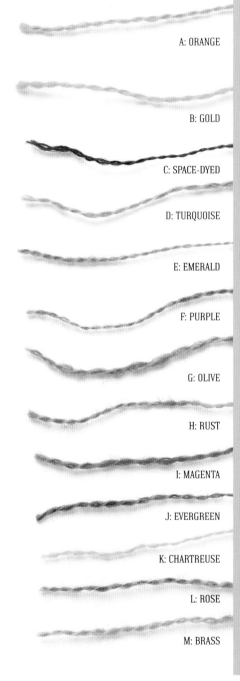

A: ORANGE

B: GOLD

C: SPACE-DYED

D: TURQUOISE

E: EMERALD

F: PURPLE

G: OLIVE

H: RUST

I: MAGENTA

J: EVERGREEN

K: CHARTREUSE

L: ROSE

M: BRASS

and D, knit across 13 held sts of left corner triangle; and with a fifth dpn and D, pick up and knit 17 sts along center triangle selvedge to I-cord at bottom point—76 sts; 38 sts each in F and D. Do not join for working in rnds. Working sts in their matching colors and twisting yarns at color join, knit 3 rows, beg and ending with a WS row—2 garter ridges completed. Break yarns and leave sts on needles.

Closure Flap with Buttonhole

Hold back with RS facing and garter panel at the top. Work flap in St st intarsia using 16 edge trim sts on needle directly above garter flap as foll:

ROW 1: (RS) With D, k8; with F, k8—each live st will have been worked using the opposite colors from the starting sts on the needle.

EVEN-NUMBERED ROWS 2–8: Purl all sts with their matching colors.

ROW 3: With D, ssk, knit to color join; with F, knit to last 2 sts, k2tog—2 sts dec'd.

ROWS 5, 7, AND 9: With E, ssk, knit to color join; with A, knit to last 2 sts, k2tog—8 sts rem after Row 9.

ROWS 10 AND 12: Rep Row 2, but *do not* cross yarns in center to create a slit opening for the buttonhole.

ROW 11: Rep Row 5, but do not cross yarns in center—6 sts rem; 3-row buttonhole slit completed; resume crossing yarns in center from this point on.

ROW 13: Rep Row 5—4 sts rem.

ROW 14: Rep Row 2.

ROW 15: With E, k1, k2tog (1 st each of E and A tog); with A, k1—3 sts rem, 2 sts E, 1 st A.

With WS facing, work all 3 sts tog with E as sssp (see Glossary)—1 st rem. Fasten off last st.

FRONT

Center Triangle

CO 16 sts with olive (G) and 16 sts with rust (H) onto a dpn so that H sts will be worked first—32 sts total. Working sts in their matching colors, work as for back center triangle, working a 3" (7.5 cm) two-color 3-st I-cord at the end.

Garter Panel

With RS facing and magenta (I), pick up 16 sts along CO edge of center triangle as for back. Knit 15 rows, beg and ending with a WS row, and changing colors as foll to make 8 garter ridges, each in a different color: 1 row I, 2 rows each B, evergreen (J), F, chartreuse (K), E, A, rose (L). Break yarn and place sts on hold.

Right and Left Corner Triangles

Using D for right corner and I for left corner, work as for back.

Front Decorative Flap

Hold front with RS facing and center triangle pointing up. With I and RS facing, beg 8 sts before center join, pick up and knit 8 sts along purl bumps from set-up row of center triangle, then with D pick up and knit 8 more sts after join—16 sts. Using I and D throughout, work Rows 2–15 as for back closure flap, crossing the yarns on all rows to eliminate buttonhole slit—3 sts rem, 2 sts I, 1 st D. Work two-color 3-st I-cord for 2½" (6.5 cm). Break yarns and draw through rem sts to fasten off. Coil I-cord into a round bobble as shown at right and use tails threaded on a tapestry needle to tack bobble to front. Weave tails into center of I-cord.

2-Color Garter-Stitch Trim

With RS facing and E, beg at I-cord at bottom point of center triangle, pick up and knit 17 sts along selvedge to held right corner triangle sts; with a second dpn and E, knit across 13 sts from holder; with a third dpn and E, pick up and knit 8 sts across BO edge of garter panel to center, then with the same needle and brass (M), pick up and knit 8 sts to end of garter panel BO edge; with a fourth dpn and M, knit across 13 held sts of left corner triangle; and with a fifth dpn and M, pick up and knit 17 sts along center triangle selvedge to I-cord—76 sts; 38 sts each in E and M. Work 2 garter ridges as for back. Break yarns and leave sts on needles.

FINISHING

Join Front to Back and Make Strap

CO 3 sts with C, leaving a long tail for attaching embellishments later. Work a 3" (7.5 cm) I-cord. Continue working I-cord while joining front and back as foll:

ROW 1: With RS of front facing, sl first st at bottom point of front to beg of I-cord sts on needle; with RS of back facing, sl first st at bottom point of back to end of I-cord sts on needle; k2tog (I-cord st tog with front st), k1, k2tog (I-cord st tog with 1 back st)—1 st joined from both front and back.

ROW 2: Work 1 row I-cord without joining. Rep the last 2 rows sixteen more times to join all 17 live sts from sides of center triangles. Continuing as established, join 13 live sts of front and back corner triangles in the same manner. Place 16 sts on needle above front garter panel on holder. Work I-cord without joining for 30" (76 cm) or desired length for strap.

Resume working joined I-cord to join live sts of rem corner triangles and sides of center triangles—16 sts in center of top front edge rem on hold; all other sts around edges of front and back have been joined. Work I-cord without joining for about 3" (7.5 cm). Cut yarn, leaving a long tail to attach embellishments. Knot the end securely and weave it back into the center of the I-cord. Attach embellishments to the starting end of the joining I-cord in the same manner.

Place 16 held sts at top edge of front on needle and join K with RS facing. Knit 1 RS row, then BO all sts as if to knit on next WS row. Tie the 5" (12.5 cm) back I-cord in an overhand knot around the base of all lower 4 I-cords, snugging the knot close against the bottom of the purse as shown. Sew larger shank button to garter panel pick-up row in center of back. Fold closure flap to front and sew smaller button to front underneath buttonhole in flap. Weave in ends. Knot strap to adjust length if desired. Full purse slightly in hot, soapy water, agitating by hand and alternating hot and cold water, for about 5 minutes. Lay flat to dry.

Lining

Fold lining fabric in half with WS out and trace the outline of purse. Trace another line ½" (1.3 cm) outside the first line and cut along outer line. With RS tog, sew lining pieces tog with a ½" (1.3 cm) seam allowance, leaving 3" (7.5 cm) opening in the center of the top. Fold edges on each side of opening ½" (1.3 cm) to WS and stitch in place. Insert lining into purse with wrong sides of purse and lining touching and slip-stitch lining in place around the purse opening, about ¼" (6 mm) down from the edge.

moth mittens

{Sarah Anderson}

The design on the back of these Norwegian-style mittens represents metamorphosis—a symbol of renewal and new life—with a caterpillar, a row of five cocoons, and a moth at the top. The motif on the palm is a reminder of one of Sarah Anderson's favorite verses from Isaiah: ". . . I shall not forget you. Look, I have inscribed you on the palms of my hands. . . ." Because the project was small and required only one skein of each yarn, Sarah wound each singles into a center-pull ball and plied from both ends.

Spinning Notes

Fiber: 2 oz (57 g) black Bluefaced Leicester top, 2 oz (57 g) orange carded roving.

Shown here: Ashland Bay black top; Alpine Meadow Fibers "Alpine Sunset" roving.

Drafting method: Short draw.

Wheel system: Direct drive.

Ratio (singles/plying): 9:1.

Singles direction spun: Z.

Singles wraps per inch: 24.

Number of plies: 2.

Plied direction spun: S.

Plied wraps per inch: 12.

Plied twists per inch: 6.

Total yardage: 296 (271 m).

Yards per pound: 1,185.

Knitting Notes

Yarn classification: Worsted weight (Medium #4).

Yardage used: 92 (94, 97) yd (84 [86, 89] m) of black and 103 (105, 107) yd (94 [96, 98] m) of alpine.

Needles: U.S. sizes 2 (2.75 mm) and 3 (3.25 mm): set of 5 double-pointed (dpn). Adjust needle sizes if necessary to obtain the correct gauge.

Gauge: 28 sts and 29 rows = 4" (10 cm) on smaller needles.

Notions: Stitch markers (m); stitch holder or smooth waste yarn; tapestry needle.

Finished size: 7½" (19 cm) hand circumference for all sizes; 10½ (11, 11½)" (26.5 [28, 29] cm) long. To fit a woman's size S (M, L).

Key

- ☐ alpine
- ▣ black
- ☐ pattern repeat
- ━ work as indicated for small
- ━ work as indicated for medium
- ━ work as indicated for large

Hand

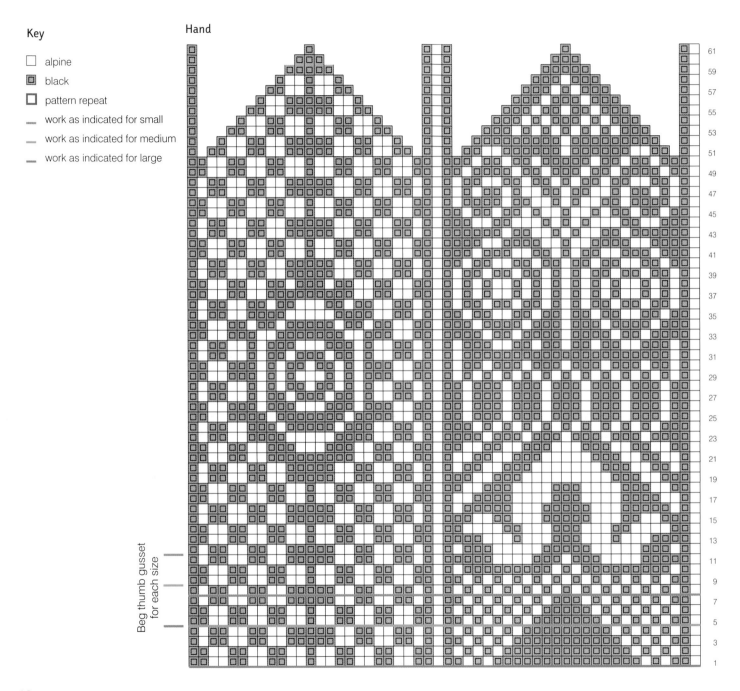

Beg thumb gusset for each size

61
59
57
55
53
51
49
47
45
43
41
39
37
35
33
31
29
27
25
23
21
19
17
15
13
11
9
7
5
3
1

18

RIGHT MITTEN

With black and larger needles, CO 52 sts. Arrange over 3 dpns, place marker (pm), and join for working in the rnd, being careful not to twist sts.

RNDS 1–3: With black, purl.

RND 4: With alpine, knit.

RNDS 5–20: Work Rnds 1–16 of Cuff chart.

RND 21: With alpine, knit.

RND 22: With black, knit.

RND 23: Purl.

RND 24: With smaller needles and alpine, knit.

RND 25: Purl.

Hand

Rearrange sts as foll: Needle 1—26 sts; Needles 2 and 3—13 sts each. Beginning with Rnd 8 (5, 1), work Hand chart.

Thumb Gusset

Following Hand chart, begin thumb gusset on 5th rnd as foll:

RND 1: Needle 1—work 5th (9th, 12th) rnd of Hand chart; Needle 2—work 3 sts from Hand chart, pm, with alpine, M1 (see Glossary), pm, work Hand chart to end; Needle 3—work Hand chart—1 st inc'd.

RND 2: Work Hand chart to first m, work Thumb Gusset chart (see page 20) to second m, and work Hand chart to end of rnd.

Rep Rnd 2 sixteen more times—17 sts between m.

NEXT RND: Needle 1—work Hand chart; Needle 2—work 3 sts from Hand chart, place 17 sts on hold for thumb, work Hand chart to end; Needle 3—work Hand chart.

Cuff

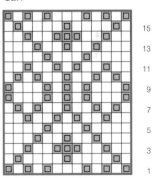

Key

☐ alpine

▣ black

Thumb Gusset

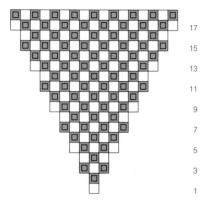

17
15
13
11
9
7
5
3
1

Hand
Work Hand chart through Rnd 50.

Top shaping
RND 51: Needle 1—with alpine, k1; with black, ssk; work Hand chart to last 2 sts, with black, k2tog; Needle 2—with alpine, k1; with black, ssk; work Hand chart to end; Needle 3—work Hand chart to last 2 sts; with black, k2tog.

Work in patt as established, working Hand chart and decreasing as on Rnd 51, ten more times—8 sts rem. Cut yarn, and draw tail through rem sts, and fasten off on WS.

Thumb
Replace 17 held thumb sts on smaller needles and pick up and knit (see Glossary) 5 sts at base of thumb, maintaining color patt—22 sts.

NEXT RND: (dec rnd) Work in patt as established to last 6 sts, [k2tog] three times in patt—19 sts rem. Rearrange sts as needed.

Continue in established color pattern until thumb measures 1½–2¼" (3.8–5.5 cm) or desired length from picked-up sts.

NEXT RND: (dec rnd) [K2tog] to last st, k1—10 sts rem.

NEXT RND: (dec rnd) [K2tog] to end—5 sts rem.

Cut yarn, draw tail through rem sts, and fasten off on WS.

LEFT MITTEN

Work as for right mitten to Thumb Gusset, reversing thumb placement. The left mitten thumb placement mark is 2 sts in from the end of Needle 3.

Thumb Gusset

Following Hand chart, begin thumb gusset on 5th rnd:

RND 1: Needle 1—work 5th (9th, 12th) rnd of Hand chart; Needle 2—work Hand chart; Needle 3—work Hand chart to last 2 sts, pm, with alpine, M1, pm, work Hand chart to end—1 st inc'd.

RND 2: Work Hand chart to first m, work Thumb chart to second m, and work Hand chart to end of rnd.

Rep Rnd 2 sixteen more times—17 sts between m.

NEXT RND: Needles 1 and 2—work Hand chart; Needle 3—work Hand chart to m, place 17 sts on hold for thumb, work Hand chart to end.

Work as for right mitten to end.

FINISHING

Weave in ends and wet block. Lay flat to dry.

21

self-striping socks

{Kathleen Taylor}

It's easy to spin self-striping yarns by Navajo-plying the singles, but what if your fiber just doesn't want to be spun that fine? Kathleen Taylor spun a two-ply self-striping yarn and knitted a basic sock pattern for colorfully functional socks. She divided the roving into its component colors, then spun a slightly thick-and-thin yarn for a pair of fraternal twin socks. The yarn has a tweedy effect where the yarn changes color gradually.

Spinning Notes

Fiber: 6.4 oz (181 g) Corriedale roving.

Shown here: Hand-dyed roving from Decadent Fibers.

Preparation: Semiworsted.

Drafting method: Short-draw.

Wheel system: Scotch tension.

Ratio (singles/plying): 6:1 (both).

Singles direction spun: S.

Singles twists per inch: 18–22 (thick and thin).

Singles wraps per inch: 20–22 (thick and thin).

Twist angle: 35°.

Number of plies: 2.

Plied direction spun: Z.

Plied twists per inch: 14–18 (thick and thin).

Plied wraps per inch: 14–16 (thick and thin).

Total yardage: 400 yd (366 m).

Yards per pound: 1,000.

Knitting Notes

Yarn classification: Sportweight (Fine #2).

Yardage used: 222 (225, 232, 335, 343, 350) yd (203 [206, 212, 306, 314, 320] m).

Needles: U.S. size 2 (3 mm): set of 5 double-pointed (dpn). U.S. size 3 (3.25 mm): set of 5 dpn. Adjust needle size if necessary to obtain the correct gauge.

Notions: Stitch markers (m); stitch holders (optional); tapestry needle.

Gauge: 14 sts and 18 rnds = 2" (5 cm).

Pattern Sizes: To fit women's 5–6 (7–8, 9–10, men's 9–10, 11–12, 13) shoe size.

Finished Sizes: 3¾ (4¼)" (9.5 [11] cm) wide; 6½ (7½)" (16.5 [19] cm) cuff length; 8¼ (8¾, 9¾, 10, 11, 12)" (21 [22, 25, 25.5, 28, 30.5] cm) from back of heel to toe.

Note: Directions are given for multiple sizes. When only one number is given, work direction for all sizes. When only two numbers are given, work the first for women's sizes and the second for men's sizes.

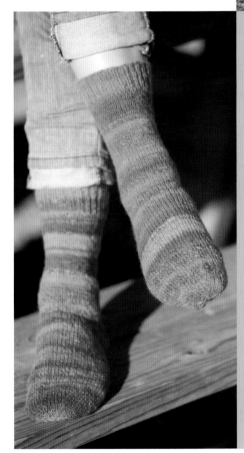

ROW 1: (WS) Sl 1 purlwise (pwise) with yarn in front (wyf), purl to end.

ROW 2: (RS) *Sl 1 pwise with yarn in back (wyb), k1; rep from * to end.

Rep Rows 1–2 until the heel flap measures 2 (2½)" (5 [6.5] cm), ending after Row 1.

HEEL

Work short-rows (see Glossary) to shape heel as foll:

Men's sizes only

SHORT-ROW 1: (RS) Sl1, k18, k2tog, k1, turn.

SHORT-ROW 2: (WS) Sl1, p9, p2tog, p1, turn.

SHORT-ROW 3: Sl 1, knit to 1 st before gap created on last row, k2tog, k1, turn.

SHORT-ROW 4: Sl 1, purl to 1 st before gap created on last row, p2tog, p1, turn.

Rep Short-rows 3–4 until all sts have been worked—18 sts rem. *Note:* On last 2 short-rows, omit k1 or p1 after dec if necessary.

GUSSET SET-UP: Sl 1, k8; rnd begins at center of heel. Redistribute sts evenly on needles.

Women's sizes only

SHORT-ROW 1: (RS) Sl 1, k14, k2tog, k1, turn.

SHORT-ROW 2: Sl 1, p5, p2tog, p1, turn.

SHORT-ROW 3: (RS) Sl 1, knit to 1 st before gap created on last row, k2tog, k1, turn.

SHORT-ROW 4: (WS) Sl 1, purl to 1 st before gap created on last row, p2tog, p1, turn.

Rep Short-rows 3–4 until all sts have been worked—14 sts rem. *Note:* On last 2 short-rows, omit k1 or p1 after dec if necessary.

GUSSET SET-UP: Sl 1, k6; rnd begins at center of heel. Redistribute sts evenly on needles.

CUFF

With larger needles, CO 54 (60) sts. Join for working in the rnd, being careful not to twist sts. Note the position of the CO in the color repeat so that you begin the second sock in the same place.

With smaller needles, work 15 (20) rnds of [k1, p1] ribbing.

LEG

Work in St st until piece measures 6½ (7½)" (16.5 [19] cm) from CO.

HEEL FLAP

SET-UP RND: K13 (15), knit the next 28 (30) sts and sl them to a holder or spare needle, knit the remaining 13 (15) sts, then knit the first 13 (15) sts, turn. These 26 (30) sts will be worked back and forth for the heel.

GUSSET

RND 1: K7 (9), pick up and knit (see Glossary) 15 (19) sts along edge of heel flap, place marker (pm), knit held instep sts, pm, pick up and knit 15 (19) sts other edge of heel flap, k7 (9)—72 (86) sts.

RND 2: Knit to 2 sts before m, k2tog, knit to m, ssk, knit to end—2 sts dec'd.

RND 3: Knit.

Rep Rnds 2–3 until 54 (60) sts rem.

FOOT

Work even until foot measures 5½ (6, 6½, 7, 8, 9)" (14 [15, 16.5, 18, 20.5, 23] cm) from heel flap edge.

TOE

Men's sizes only

RND 1: *K8, k2tog; rep from * to end—54 sts rem.

RND 2 AND ALL EVEN-NUMBERED RNDS: Knit.

RND 3: *K7, k2tog; rep from * to end—48 sts rem.

RNDS 4–13: Continue as established, working 1 fewer st between decreases on each dec rnd—18 sts rem after Rnd 13.

RND 14: *K1, k2tog; rep from * to end—12 sts rem.

Women's sizes only

Work Rnds 3–14 as for men's sizes.

FINISHING

Cut yarn, leaving a 12" (30.5 cm) tail. With tail threaded on a tapestry needle, draw through rem sts and pull tight. Fasten off on the inside of the sock.

Weave in all ends. Wash and block.

 Spinning Self-Striping Two-Ply

Kathleen examined her handpainted roving for long areas of single (or mostly single) colors and found many 30" (76 cm) lengths of all three colors in the roving. She pulled the roving apart at the color separations and set the lengths in piles of single colors for six 30" (76 cm) strips each of orange, pumpkin, and rust. She then gathered one strip of each color and tied them together loosely in a bundle until she had six bundles. The smaller bundles made it easier to maintain the striping pattern, although they required more joining while knitting. She divided each piece of roving in each bundle lengthwise and spun one-half of each bundle in order from lightest to darkest for each of two bobbins of slightly thick-and-thin singles, then plied each pair of bobbins.

andean alpaca poncho

{Kaye D. Collins}

Soft and silky, this comfortable hooded poncho is easy to drop over a baby's head. Warm enough for winter wear, it is inspired by Peruvian textiles. High in the Andes, the men and children wear warm hats and ponchos woven on backstrap looms. This poncho features an authentic Andean *punta* scalloped edging worked in several natural shades of alpaca spun with tighter twist. Alpacas are embroidered in natural colors along the bottom edge in thicker yarn. Tassels are added at bottom edge corners, neck cord ends, and the top of the hood.

Spinning Notes

Fiber: Poncho—7 oz (199 g) raw white alpaca and 3 oz (85 g) prepared white 19-micron Merino blended 3 times on drumcarder. Puntas and Alpacas—less than ¼ oz (7 g) 100% alpaca in three or more natural shades, drumcarded.

Preparation: Washed alpaca, drumcarded once, then blended with Merino. Batts torn into strips and predrafted.

Drafting method: Poncho and Alpacas—semiwoolen. Puntas—short draw.

Wheel system: Scotch tension.

Ratio (singles/plying): 17:1.

Singles direction spun: Z.

Singles twists per inch: 7.

Singles wraps per inch: Poncho—28.

Number of plies: Poncho and Puntas—2. Alpacas—3.

Plied direction spun: S.

Plied twists per inch: Poncho—3.5. Puntas—4. Alpacas—3.

Plied wraps per inch: Poncho—14. Puntas—15. Alpacas—10.

Total yardage: Poncho—500 yd (457 m). Puntas—40 yd (37 m). Alpacas—25 yd (23 m).

Yards per pound: Poncho—1,150. Puntas—2,594. Alpacas—1,621.

Knitting Notes

Yarn classification: Poncho and Puntas—Sportweight (Fine #2). Alpacas—Worsted weight (Medium #4).

Yardage used: Poncho—400 yd (366 m). Puntas—20 yd (18 m). Alpacas—18 yd (16 m).

Needles: U.S. size 5 (3.75 mm): 29" (73.5 cm) circular (cir). U.S. size 3 (3.25 mm): 7" (18 cm) double-pointed (dpn) or cir. Adjust needle size if necessary to obtain the correct gauge.

Hook: U.S. sizes K/10½ (6.5 mm), D/3 (3.25 mm), and B/1 (2.25 mm).

Notions: Stitch markers (m), 21 in one color and 1 in another color for beg of rnd; tapestry needle.

Gauge: 24 sts and 32 rows = 4" (10 cm).

Finished size: 20" (51 cm) wide at hem and 18" (45.5 cm) long from hem to top of hood. Fits sizes 3 months to 1 year.

PONCHO

CO 240 sts. Place different-colored marker (pm) for beg of rnd and join for working in the rnd, being careful not to twist sts.

RND 1: Purl.

RNDS 2–9: Knit.

RND 10: [K60, place marker] three times, k60.

RND 11: (dec rnd) *K1, k2tog, knit to 3 sts before next m, ssk, k1; rep from * to end—232 sts rem.

RNDS 12–14: Knit.

RND 15: Repeat Rnd 11—224 sts rem.

RND 16: Purl.

RND 17: Knit.

RND 18: Repeat Rnd 11—216 sts rem.

RNDS 19–20: Knit.

Rep Rnds 17–20 five more times—176 sts rem.

Remove 3 m, leaving only m for beg of rnd. Knit until piece measures 7" (18 cm) from CO edge.

Neck opening

Work back and forth in rows, dividing for neck at remaining m. Slipping first st pwise wyb on each RS row and wyf on WS on each row, work in St st until piece measures 8½" (21.5 cm) from CO edge, ending after a WS row.

Shoulder Decreases

SET-UP ROW: [K8, pm] ten times, k8, pm for center of back, [k8, pm] ten times, k8.

ROW 1 AND ALL WS ROWS: Purl.

ROW 2: Sl 1, k5, k2tog, [k6, k2tog] ten times, [ssk, k6] eleven times—154 sts rem.

ROW 4: Sl 1, k4, k2tog, [k5, k2tog] ten times, [ssk, k5] eleven times—132 sts rem.

Continue as established, working 1 fewer st between decreases on each dec rnd, for four more rows—88 sts rem after Row 8.

Neck Ribbing
ROW 1: (RS) K3, *p2, k2; rep from * to last 3 sts, k3.
ROW 2: P3, *k2, p2; rep from * to last 3 sts, p3.
ROW 3: (eyelet row) K3, *k2tog, yo, k2; rep from * to last 3 sts, k3.
ROW 4: Rep Row 2.
ROW 5: Rep Row 1.

Hood
Work in St st, slipping first st of every row, until hood measures 7" (18 cm) from top of ribbing, ending after a RS row.
NEXT ROW: P44 sts.
Holding RS of hood tog, use the three-needle method (see Glossary) to join top of hood.

FINISHING
Weave in loose ends. Block.

Cord
With 1 strand of each color held tog and largest hook, make a 36" (91.5 cm) crochet chain (see Glossary). Thread cord through eyelets in ribbing.

Tassels
Using the punta yarns plus white together, make seven 1¾" (4.5 cm) tassels (see Glossary). Attach to top of hood, cord edges, and corners at bottom edge.

Duplicate Stitch

With yarn for alpacas threaded on a tapestry needle, use duplicate st and straight st (see Glossary) to embroider alpacas evenly spaced across lower edge so that they face each other at the center front and alternating colors as desired; repeats were spaced 4 sts apart, with 8 sts between repeats at each corner.

Hood Trim

Trim hood edge with Andean punta edging or crochet picot trim.

punta edging

(multiple of 6 sts + 1)
The punta (or point) is a scalloped edging borrowed from authentic edgings that decorate the colorful Andean hats. It is knitted separately and sewn on the finished poncho hood.

With U.S. size D/3 (3.25 mm) hook and gray yarn, ch 163 sts; draw tail through loop to bind off.

Attach black yarn to beg of chain with a loose knot. Using size B/1 (2.25 mm) hook and black, pick up and knit 1 st in the bump on the underside of each ch and place on double-pointed knitting needle all the way across, being careful not to twist sts.

Attach brown yarn to knot at beg of row. *Sl 1, k4; sl 2 sts purlwise (pwise) with yarn in back (wyb) from right needle back to left needle, k2tog (4 sts on right needle), k1, sl

Alpaca Embroidery

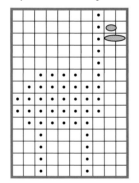
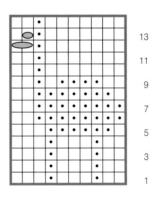

⊡	duplicate st
⬭	straight st over 2 sts
⬭	straight st over 1 st
☐	repeat

13
11
9
7
5
3
1

3 sts from right needle to left needle, pass 2nd and 3rd sts over first st (1 st on left needle); knit first st again, k1 from left needle—4 sts on left needle (1 black, 3 brown); 7 sts dec'd to 4; 1 punta completed. Rep from * twenty-two more times, sl rem st—23 puntas; 93 sts rem. Turn.

With black, purl 2 rows. BO kwise. Cut yarn and draw through last loop. Weave in ends. Pin punta to edge of hood with ends at top of ribbing, and sew to the outside of hood edge.

tips

- If you find it difficult to pick up the bumps, try folding the chain in half against itself; the bumps will pop up.
- Be careful not to twist stitches when placing them on the double-pointed needle.
- If needed, use a point protector to prevent sts from slipping off needle.

crochet picot

This crocheted 3 st edging is a simpler method for the hood edging. (See Glossary for crochet directions.)

ROW 1: With RS of hood facing, black, and size D/3 (3.25 mm) hook, and beg at bottom right of hood, sc in both loops of each edge st to bottom left of hood. Do not turn.

ROW 2: With brown, *sc in first sc, sc in second sc, ch 3 sts, sc in next sc; rep from * to bottom left of hood.

wisteria lace shawl
{Diane Mulholland}

This small shawl shows off fine handspun yarn beautifully with a simple lace design. A small wandering eyelet pattern flows into the larger border stitch, and the shawl is finished with an elegant scalloped edge. The shawl pattern was inspired by the wisteria in a neighbor's garden that matched the color of the fiber perfectly. With such a large project, Diane Mulholland kept her control card handy to ensure even grist.

Spinning Notes

Fiber: 3¼ oz (92 g) Polwarth lamb's fleece, weighed after preparation.

Preparation: Washed lock by lock, dyed in individual locks, and flick carded.

Drafting method: Semiworsted, from the corner of each flicked lock.

Wheel system: Scotch tension.

Ratio (singles/plying): 14:1.

Singles direction spun: S.

Singles wraps per inch: 50.

Number of plies: 2.

Plied direction spun: Z.

Plied twists per inch: 8.

Plied wraps per inch: 27.

Total yardage: 600 yd (549 m).

Yards per pound: 3,033.

Knitting Notes

Yarn classification:: Laceweight (Lace #0).

Yardage used: 600 yd (549 m).

Needles: U.S. size 5 (3.75 mm)—32" (80 cm) circular (cir). Adjust needle size if necessary to obtain the correct gauge. *Note:* Shawl may be started on straight needles and transferred to circular needle when there are too many stitches to continue on straights.

Gauge: Not critical for this project. For shawl shown, 32 sts and 48 rows (4 patt reps wide and 3 patt reps high) of Wandering Lace chart measure about 5¾" (14.5 cm) wide and 4¾" (12 cm) high, relaxed after blocking.

Notions: Stitch markers (m); blocking pins; tapestry needle.

Finished size: 60" (152.5 cm) wide across top edge and 30" (76 cm) from center of top edge to lower point, relaxed after blocking.

33

❖ NOTES

The shawl begins in the center of the top edge with an I-cord edging at each side, then stitches are increased inside the I-cord edgings and on each side of the center stitch on RS rows to produce a triangle shape.

Only RS rows are shown on charts. For WS rows, work 3-st WS I-cord edging row (see Stitch Guide), purl to last 3 sts, work 3-st WS I-cord edging row.

To adjust the finished size, work more or fewer pairs of repeats of the Wandering Lace chart. Every two 16-row repeats added or removed will change the "wingspan" measurement across the top edge by about 11" to 12" (28 to 30.5 cm) and the length from top edge to lower point by about 5½" to 6" (14 to 15 cm). Plan on spinning more yarn if making a larger shawl.

Alternatively, use a heavier or lighter yarn with an appropriate needle size for a larger or smaller shawl.

Each time you repeat the Wandering Lace chart enough stitches will be added to work two more 8-st repeats in each half. For example, when you work the chart the first time there will only be enough stitches to work each marked repeat section twice. Because the stitch count increases by 2 stitches in each half every RS row, or 16 stitches in each half every 16 rows, the second time you work the chart there will be enough stitches to work each 8-stitch pattern repeat four times, and the following time you work the chart there will be enough stitches to work each 8-st repeat six times, and so on.

34

SHAWL

Using a provisional method (see Glossary), CO 3 sts. Work 4 rows of regular I-cord (see Glossary).

SET-UP ROW: (RS) K3, with RS still facing, pick up and knit 3 sts along edge of I-cord, remove provisional CO, place 3 revealed sts on left needle, k3—9 sts.

NEXT ROW: (WS) Sl 3 pwise wyf, p2, pm, p1, sl 3 pwise wyf.

Work Rows 1–20 of Foundation Chart (see Notes, page 34, and Stitch Guide for working I-cord edging)—49 sts. Rep Rows 1–16 of Wandering Lace chart seven times—273 sts. If making a larger or smaller shawl (see Notes), work more or fewer reps of Wandering Lace chart, making sure to work an odd number of reps total so the st count is a multiple of 32 sts plus 17 for a smooth transition to the next chart.

NEXT ROW: (RS) Work Row 1 of Wisteria Border Right Half chart across first 137 sts, then work Row 1 of Wisteria Border Left Half over 136 sts—4 sts inc'd; 277 sts total after completing Row 1.

Work Rows 2–42 of Wisteria Border charts as established—357 sts.

NEXT ROW: Work Row 1 of Scalloped Edging Right Half chart across 179 sts, then work Row 1 of Scalloped Edging Left Half over 178 sts—4 sts inc'd; 361 sts after completing Row 1.

Work Rows 2–13 of Scalloped Edging chart, ending with a RS row (do not work a WS row after final row of this chart); Rows 9–13 of chart do not add sts on each side of center st—379 sts.

With WS facing, BO as foll: P3tog, *k1, sl 2 sts back to left needle and k2tog through back loops (tbl); rep from * to last 3 sts, k3tog, sl 2 sts back to left needle, k2tog tbl, cut yarn, draw tail through rem st, and fasten off.

FINISHING

Weave in all ends but do not trim flush with surface of shawl yet. Soak in warm water with a little fiber rinse for about 15 minutes. Remove carefully, supporting the weight of the shawl, and squeeze out excess water by rolling in a towel. Block to about 65" (165 cm) across top edge and 35" (89 cm) from center of top edge to lower point, pinning out points at each [yo, k1, yo] in last chart row along two long sides; finished piece will relax to about 60" (152.5 cm) wide and 30" (76 cm) high. Allow to dry completely. Trim ends.

 stitch guide I-Cord Edging

ALL RS ROWS: K3, sl 3 sts back to left needle and work them again as k3, work in pattern to last 3 sts, k3, sl 3 sts back to left needle and work them again as k3.

ALL WS ROWS: Sl 3 sts as if to purl with yarn in front (pwise wyf), purl to last 3 sts, sl 3 sts pwise wyf.

Foundation

19
17
15
13
11
9
7
5
3
1

↑
center st

Wandering Lace

15
13
11
9
7
5
3
1

↑
center st

Key

knit

○ yo

╱ k2tog

╲ ssk

⋏ sl 1 kwise, k2tog, psso

I I-cord edging
(see Stitch Guide)

no stitch

pattern repeat

I marker position

Wisteria Border Right Half

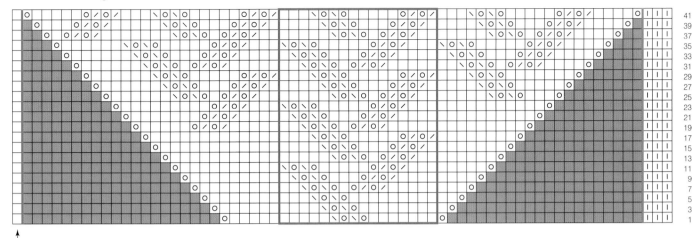

↑ center st

Wisteria Border Left Half

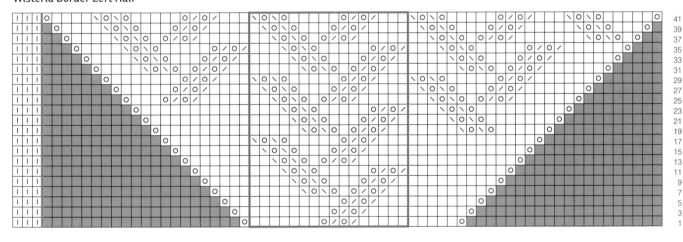

WISTERIA LACE SHAWL

Scalloped Edging Right Half

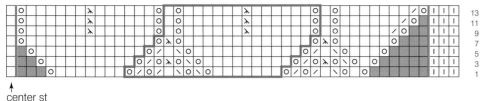

13
11
9
7
5
3
1

center st

Scalloped Edging Left Half

13
11
9
7
5
3
1

Key

☐ knit

○ yo

╱ k2tog

╲ ssk

⋏ sl 1 kwise, k2tog, psso

❘ I-cord edging (see Stitch Guide)

▧ no stitch

☐ pattern repeat

❘ marker position

✳ Washing Locks

Diane washed each Polwarth lock individually in small batches. She found the process of washing the fleece in locks "laborious (yet gloriously fulfilling)." Working in small batches, she folded the locks inside squares of cheesecloth, making parcels that fit into pans, then soaked them for a while in very hot water and dish detergent. Experience taught her that ultimate care was needed to avoid felting the cut end of this very fine fleece, and the parcels were left to drain without squeezing or rolling. Another soak, a rinse or two, and finally a roll in a towel to press out the moisture, and the locks were unwrapped and laid out to dry. The perfectly preserved clean locks needed little preparation for spinning; flicking open the ends of each left it ready to spin with a semiworsted draft. Like many spinners who process fleece at home, Diane finds that spinning after such thorough preparation is almost always an enjoyable and relaxing process.

38

WISTERIA LACE SHAWL

zipped baby hoodie

{Lisa Shroyer; yarn by Nancy Shroyer}

When Nancy Shroyer's children were babies, she found that a sweater with a back zipper made it easy to slip on. One of those babies, Lisa, grew into an editor and knitwear designer, and the duo decided to create a new interpretation of the favorite silhouette. The two-ply sportweight yarn pairs one strand of cool tones and one of warm tones in a bright, clear palette. The mitered garter squares show off the colors of the yarn and celebrate their tendency to stripe.

Spinning Notes

Fiber: 7 oz (198 g) superwash Merino.

Shown here: Fiber from The Mannings Studio, dyed with Country Classics dyes.

Drafting method: From the fold.

Wheel system: Scotch tension.

Singles direction spun: Z.

Singles twists per inch: 14.

Singles wraps per inch: 18.

Plied direction spun: S.

Number of plies: 2.

Plied twists per inch: 7.

Plied wraps per inch: 14.

Total yardage: 495 yd (453 m).

Yards per pound: 1,133.

Knitting Notes

Yarn classification: Sportweight (Fine #2).

Yardage used: 353 (450) yd (323 [411] m).

Needles: U.S. size 5 (3.75 mm): 24" (60 cm) circular (cir) and set 5 of double-pointed (dpn). Adjust needle size if necessary to obtain the correct gauge.

Gauge: 19½ sts and 26 rows = 4" (10 cm) in St st.

Notions: Stitch markers (m); waste yarn or spare cir needles for stitch holders; tapestry needle; U.S. size F/5 (3.75 mm) crochet hook; 12 (16)" polyester zipper (not a jacket zipper); sewing needle and matching thread.

Finished size: 20 (24)" (51 [61] cm) chest circumference; to fit a 12-month-old (18-month-old). Sweater shown in smaller size.

41

SWEATER

Bottom band

With cir needle, CO 130 (148) sts.

ROW 1: (WS) Knit.

Working in garter st (knit every row), shape ends with mitered corners as foll:

ROW 2: (RS) K14, sl 1, k2tog, psso, knit to last 17 sts, sl 1, k2tog, psso, knit to end—4 sts dec'd; 126 (144) sts rem.

ROW 3: (WS) Knit.

ROW 4: K13, sl 1, k2tog, psso, knit to last 16 sts, sl 1, k2tog, psso, knit to end—4 sts dec'd.

ROW 5: Knit.

Work in patt as established, shaping corners by working 1 fewer st before and after dec's on each RS row and knitting each WS row, thirteen more times, ending after a WS row—1 st rem outside centered dec st at each end; 70 (88) sts rem.

NEXT ROW: (RS) K2tog, knit to last 2 sts, k2tog—68 (86) sts rem. Break yarn.

NEXT ROW: (RS) Join yarn to end of band (top selvedge corner of mitered corner, level with sts at center of row); pick up and knit (see Glossary) 15 sts to beg of live sts, k68 (86), pick up and knit 15 sts across open selvedge of mitered corner—98 (116) sts. Row spans top width of bottom band.

Body

ROW 1: (WS) P2, k1, purl to last 3 sts, k1, p2.

ROW 2: (RS) K2, p1, knit to last 3 sts, p1, k2.

Rep Rows 1 and 2 until body measures 7¼ (7¾)" (18.5 [19.5] cm) from bottom of band or 4 (4½)" (10 [11.5] cm) from top of band, ending after a WS row.

armholes

NEXT ROW: (RS) Work 22 (26) sts in patt, BO 4 sts, work 46 (56) sts in patt, BO 4 sts, work last 22 (26) sts in patt—90 (108)

NOTES

This sweater is worked from the bottom up. The zipper is placed in the back of the sweater and runs from hem to the top of the hood. The zipper closes from top to bottom, allowing easy off and on, and is already "hooked" when sewn in. The open back avoids pulling a tight neckline over a baby's head.

The bottom band of the sweater is shaped with mitered corners at the back opening, and the hood is worked as two mitered squares with a short-row-shaped garter-stitch wedge at the top of the hood. The mitered squares show off a hand-dyed roving or striped yarn nicely.

42

sts rem, 22 (26) sts for each back and 46 (56) sts for front. Place body sts on hold.

Sleeves

With dpns, CO 35 (39) sts. Place marker (pm) and join for working in the rnd, being careful not to twist sts.

RND 1: Knit.

RND 2: Purl.

Rep Rnds 1 and 2 two more times. Work in St st until piece measures 6 (6½)" (15 [16.5] cm) from CO.

NEXT RND: (BO for underarm) Knit to last 2 sts of rnd, BO last 2 sts of rnd, BO first 2 sts of next rnd—31 (35) sts rem.

Place sts on hold and work second sleeve.

Yoke

With RS of all pieces facing, join pieces as foll: Work 22 (26) sts of left back, k31 (35) of one sleeve onto cir needle, k46 (56) of front, k31 (35) of second sleeve, work 22 (26) sts of right back in patt—152 (178) sts total. Do not join for working in the rnd.

NEXT ROW: (WS) Work 22 (26) sts in patt, pm, p31 (35), pm, p46 (56), pm, p31 (35), pm, work 22 (26) sts in patt.

Shape raglan

Note: Read through the following directions before proceeding, as several actions are performed at the same time.

ROW 1: (RS; dec rnd) Work to 3 sts before m, k2tog, k1, sl m, k1, ssk, knit to 3 sts before next m, k2tog, k1, sl m, k1, ssk, knit to 3 sts before next m, k2tog, k1, sl m, k1, ssk, knit to 3 sts before next m, k2tog, k1, sl m, k1, ssk, work to end—8 sts dec'd.

ROW 2: (WS) P2, k1, p to last 3 sts, k1, p2.

Rep Rows 1 and 2 eleven (thirteen) more times—96 (112) sts eliminated at raglan lines; yoke should measure about 3¾ (4½)" (9.5 [11.5] cm) deep after all raglan decs are worked, and at the same time when

yoke measures 3 (3¾)" (7.5 [9.5] cm) from underarm (measured straight up center of front, not along the diagonal of raglan lines), shape neck as foll: BO center 6 sts of front. Working in patt as established and continuing raglan shaping, dec 1 st at each neck edge two (three) times—10 (12) sts total eliminated by neck shaping.

Work in patt to end of raglan shaping—46 (54) sts rem when all shaping is complete, 23 (27) sts rem each side of neck; 8 (10) sts for each back, 3 sts for each sleeve, 4 sts for each raglan column, 4 (6) sts for each front.

Neck

Working each side separately, work each side as foll:

Beg on WS, work 7 rows in [k1, p1] rib.

NEXT ROW: Work 2 sts, M1, work in rib to last 2 sts, M1, work last 2 sts—25 (29) sts.

Hood side panel

Knit 1 RS row. Knit 1 WS row; without turning, at end of row use backward-loop method (see Glossary) to CO 24 (28) sts—49 (57) sts.

NEXT ROW: (RS) Working across all sts, k23 (27), sl 1, k2tog, psso, knit to end—2 sts dec'd.

NEXT ROW: (WS) Knit.

NEXT ROW: (RS) K22 (26), sl 1, k2tog, psso, knit to end.

NEXT ROW: (WS) Knit.

Work in patt as established, working 1 fewer st before and after decs on each RS row, twenty-two (twenty-six) more times—1 st rem. Fasten off last st. Hood side panel should measure about 5 (5½)" (12.5 [14] cm) square. Rep for other side. When both hood panels are complete, work top hood wedge as foll: With RS of right hood side panel facing, pick up and knit 25 (29) sts along top selvedge. Knit

1 WS row. Shape with short-rows as foll (wrapping sts is not necessary in garter st):

SHORT-ROW 1: (RS) K19 (23), turn, (WS) knit to end.

Knit 2 rows across all sts.

SHORT-ROW 2: (RS) K13 (17), turn, (WS) knit to end.

Knit 2 rows.

SHORT-ROW 3: (RS) K9 (13), turn, (WS) knit to end.

Knit 2 rows.

SHORT-ROW 4: (RS) K13 (17), turn, (WS) knit to end.

Knit 2 rows.

SHORT-ROW 5: (RS) K19 (23), turn, (WS) knit to end.

Knit 2 rows. BO all sts knitwise (kwise) on RS. Use tapestry needle and mattress st (see Glossary) to sew open edges of wedge and other hood side panel tog.

FINISHING

Zipper facing: With cir needle and beg at bottom of left back bottom band, pick up and knit about 74 (80) sts along left back edge (zipper facing ends about 3" [7.5 cm] down from tip of hood), pick up and knit 2 sts at center of top hood, pick up and knit 74 sts down right back edge—150 (162) sts. (Adjust st count as necessary to avoid puckering or rippling.) Turn and purl 1 WS row. BO all sts kwise.

Neck edge: If desired, use crochet hook to work 2 rows of sl st (see Glossary) along bottom of neck edge. This creates a clean edge and firms up the neckline.

Weave in loose ends and block as desired. With sewing needle and thread, insert zipper (see Glossary) so slider closes from top to bottom, setting end of zipper 2–3" (5–7.5 cm) down from top of hood opening. Once zipper is sewn in, use yarn and tapestry needle to sew rem opening of hood closed.

43

prairie scarf

{Nancy Bush; yarn by Judith MacKenzie McCuin}

Judith MacKenzie McCuin got her first bison fiber from her husband, Nick, when they were living on a ranch in the wilds of eastern Montana that shared a fence with a herd of bison. One day Nick came home with a shirt pocket full of beautiful chocolate brown downy fibers. "Think you can spin this?" he asked. Thus began a grand adventure. The scarf, which reflects the traditional history and territory of North American Bison, was inspired by the fiber. The Little Arrowhead lace pattern forms the border, and the Estonian leaf lace pattern evokes the heads of ripe wheat.

Spinning Notes

Fiber: 3.5 oz (100 g) bison.

Preparation: Washed, dehaired, and commercially carded.

Drafting method: Semiwoolen.

Wheel system: Double drive.

Ratio (singles/plying): 10:1 (singles), 12:1 (plying).

Singles direction spun: Z.

Singles twists per inch: 10–12.

Singles wraps per inch: 42.

Twist angle: 40°.

Number of plies: 2.

Plied direction spun: S.

Plied twists per inch: 16.

Plied wraps per inch: 32.

Total yardage: 580 yd (530 m).

Yards per pound: 2,640.

Knitting Notes

Yarn classification: Laceweight (Lace #0).

Yardage used: 350 yd (320 m).

Needles: U.S. size 5 (3.75 mm): straight. Adjust needle size if necessary to obtain the correct gauge.

Notions: Stitch markers (m); U.S. size G (4.25 mm) crochet hook; 2 yd (1.8 m) cotton waste yarn; tapestry needle; blocking pins.

Gauge: 21 sts and 28 rows = 4" (10 cm) in stockinette stitch, unblocked; 24½ sts and 24 rows = 4" (10 cm) in patt from Center chart, after blocking.

Finished size: 8" (20.5 cm) wide and 72" (183 cm) long, after blocking.

Key

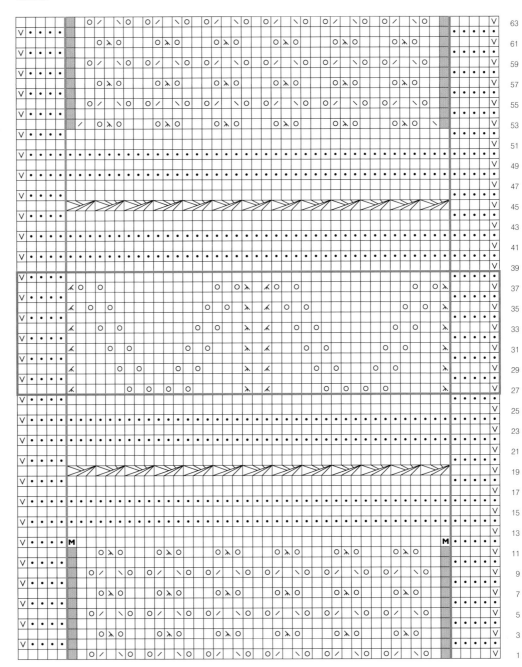

☐	knit on RS; purl on WS
•	purl on RS; knit on WS
○	yo
╱	k2tog
╲	sl 1, k1, psso
⟋	k3tog
⋏	sl 1, k2tog, psso
M	m1 (see Glossary)
V	sl 1 (see instructions)
▓	no stitch
☐	pattern repeat
￨	marker position
⧄	gathered sts *

* gathered sts
(worked over 3 sts):
K3tog but do not slip
sts from needle, yo,
then knit the same 3
sts tog again, then
slip all 3 sts from
needle.

Center

work
twenty-eight
times

Edge

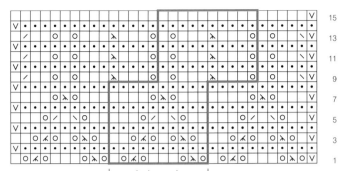

⌐ work three times ⌐

CENTER

Using crochet hook and waste yarn, use the crochet provisional method (see Glossary) to CO 47 sts. Knit 1 RS row. *Note:* Sl the first st of every row as if to purl with yarn in front (pwise wyf), then move the yarn to the back of the work between the needles before working the next st.

Work 5 rows in garter st, slipping first st of each row, and beg and ending with a WS row—3 garter ridges at beg of center section; 4th garter ridge will be added later at start of edging.

Work Rows 1–26 of Center chart, placing markers (pm) 5 sts from each end in first row as shown—49 sts after completing Row 12. Rep Rows 27–38 a total of twenty-eight times. Work Rows 39–63 once—47 sts after completing Row 63.

Work 7 rows in garter st, slipping first st of each row, beg and ending with a WS row, and at the same time, inc 4 sts evenly in last row—51 sts; 4 garter ridges at end of center section.

EDGING

Removing marker at each side as you come to it, work Rows 1–15 of Edge chart, beg and ending with a RS row. Join a second strand of yarn and BO all sts with WS facing and yarn doubled as foll: Sl 1, k1, *insert left needle into front of 2 sts just worked from left to right and k2tog, k1; rep from * to last 2 sts, k2tog, break yarn and draw through rem loop.

Carefully remove provisional CO and place 47 released sts on needle. Join yarn with WS facing and knit 1 WS row, inc 4 sts evenly across—51 sts; 4 garter ridges completed at beg of center section.

Work Rows 1–15 of Edge chart, then BO as for first edging.

FINISHING

Handwash gently in mild soap and warm water. Pin scarf to desired shape and allow to dry completely. Weave in ends.

※ Spinning Bison

Bison spinning fiber comes from one of the animal's five coats. It's an undercoat fiber, like cashmere, qiviut, or yak, and like these fibers it is naturally shed when the weather becomes warmer (although most commercially available spinning fiber is shorn from hide). The bison used for this project was washed and commercially dehaired, then made into roving. Bison is best spun using a woolen style of spinning because of the short staple and to preserve the fiber's softness. Judith spun this yarn semiwoolen, allowing the fiber to bloom, even though the lace pattern will be somewhat obscured. She let the twist run into the fiber but drafted forward toward the wheel to give the yarn more stability and better stitch definition than with a pure woolen technique. The singles is fairly loosely twisted; bison's crimp helps lock the fibers in place. This traditional two-ply lace yarn was finished by fulling: Judith immersed the skein in hot soapy water and pounded it with a small sink plunger, then rinsed the skein in icy cold water, allowing the bison fiber to bloom and become even softer.

lace-up mittens

{Sara Lamb}

These mittens were extemporaneous knitting—sitting on a plane with yarn and needles, Sara Lamb improvised these mittens, trying them on as she went. Elegant yet functional, they start with a band of lace edging that is knitted side to side from a provisional cast-on. When the lace is long enough to form into a circle that will pass easily over the wearer's fist, the edging is joined. This clever method allows for a perfectly fitting mitten with no gauge swatch.

Spinning Notes

Fiber: 5 oz (142 g) Polwarth roving.

Shown here: Natural Polwarth from Rovings, dyed as roving.

Drafting method: Long draw.

Wheel system: Scotch tension.

Ratio (singles/plying): 17:1.

Singles direction spun: Z.

Number of plies: 3.

Plied direction spun: S.

Plied twists per inch: 6.6.

Plied wraps per inch: 15.

Total yardage: 328 yd (300 m).

Yards per pound: 1,050.

Knitting Notes

Yarn classification: DK weight (Light #3).

Yardage used: 209 yd (191 m).

Needles: U.S. size 00 (1.75 mm): set of 5 double-pointed (dpn). Adjust needle size if necessary to obtain the correct gauge.

Gauge: 16 sts and 25 rnds = 2" (5 cm) in St st.

Finished size: 7" (18 cm) circumference and 11" (28 cm) from cuff to tip. To fit a woman's size small.

Notions: Waste yarn; tapestry needle; stitch markers (m); stitch holder.

49

Lace

⌢	⌢	⌢										

Key
- ☐ knit on RS; purl on WS
- ☑ sl 1 wyb on RS; sl 1 wyf on WS
- ○ yo
- ◻ ssk
- ⌢ bind off 1 st
- ▨ no stitch

Row numbers: 7, 5, 3, 1

MITTEN

Lace Edging

With crochet provisional method (see Glossary), CO 10 sts.

SET-UP ROW: Purl.

Work Rows 1–8 of Lace chart thirteen times (or long enough to circumnavigate recipient's closed fist), ending after Row 8.

Remove waste yarn from CO and place sts on one dpn. With RS held tog and beginning at bottom edge, use the three-needle method (see Glossary) to BO sts.

Cuff

Pick up and knit (see Glossary) 1 st in each sl st along edge of lace plus 1 st in CO row (53 sts for 13 reps of Lace chart). Divide sts as evenly as possible over 4 dpns. Join for working in the rnd. Work in St st for 1½" (3.8 cm).

NEXT RND: Dec 5 sts evenly (48 sts), or about 10% of total number of sts on needles, to an even number.

Ribbing

RNDS 1–12: *K1, p1; rep from * to end.
RNDS 13–14: Knit.

Thumb Gusset

RND 1: Knit to desired position of thumb, place marker (pm), M1L (see Glossary), k1, M1R (see Glossary), pm, knit to end of rnd—2 sts inc'd. (To position lace seam at the underside of the wrists, knit one-fourth of sts before thumb for left mitten and three-fourths of sts before thumb for right mitten.)

RNDS 2–3: Knit.

RND 4: Knit to m, M1L, knit to m, M1R, knit to end of rnd—2 sts inc'd.

RNDS 5–8: Knit.

Rep Rnds 4–8 seven more times—19 sts for thumb gusset; 66 sts total for 13 reps of Lace chart.

NEXT RND: Knit to m, place 19 thumb sts on hold, CO 6 sts over thumb gap, knit to end— 53 sts total for 13 reps of Lace chart.

Body

Work in St st until mitten measures about 3½" (9 cm) from thumb gusset or until knitting reaches tip of little finger. On last rnd, work evenly spaced decs as needed so that number of rem sts is divisible by 4 (for 13 reps of Lace chart, k2tog—52 sts rem).

Top

Note: For left mitten, work left-leaning (ssk) decreases; for right mitten, work right-leaning (k2tog) decreases.

RND 1: Knit, placing 4 markers evenly spaced around.

RND 2: *Work to m, dec 1; rep from * to end—4 sts dec'd.

RND 3: Knit.

Rep Rnds 2–3 four more times.

Rep Rnd 2 only until 8 sts rem. Cut yarn. Draw yarn through rem sts, pull tight, and fasten off on inside.

Thumb

Knit 19 thumb sts from holder, pm, M1, pick up and knit 8 sts at base of thumb, M1—29 sts. Arrange sts evenly over 4 dpns.

RND 1: Knit to m, k2tog, ssk, k2, [k2tog] twice—25 sts rem.

RND 2: Knit to m, k1, ssk, k2tog, k1—23 sts rem.

RND 3: Knit to m, k1, ssk, k1—22 sts rem.

Work even in St st to tip of thumb.

NEXT RND: [K3, k2tog] four times, k2—18 sts rem.

NEXT RND: [K2, k2tog] four times, k2—14 sts rem.

Continue as established, working 1 fewer st between decs on each dec rnd, until 6 sts rem. Cut yarn. Draw tail through rem sts, pull tight, and fasten off inside.

FINISHING

Weave in ends. Block mittens, pinning out lace edging to straighten the points.

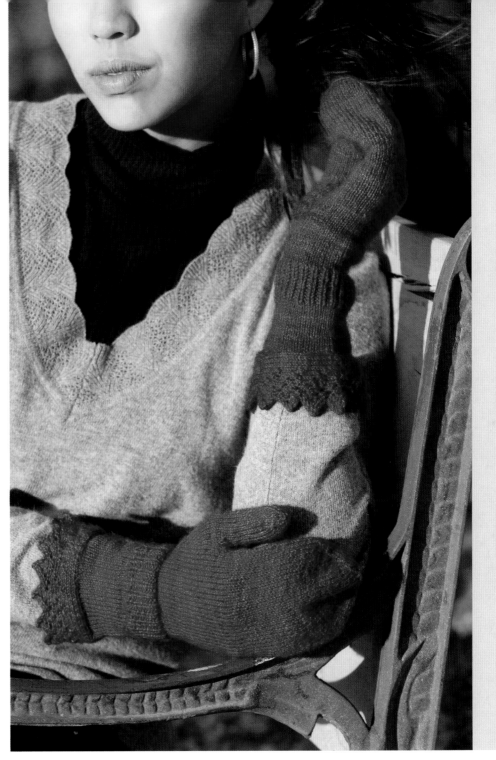

hannah's autumn jacket

{Amy Clarke Moore}

Amy designed this domino-knit sweater on the needles for her daughter, Hannah, to fit her toddler body—with her slender back and buddha belly—so the back is narrower than the front. The three-quarter-length sleeves are less likely to be dragged through applesauce and paint. To size this up with larger squares for a larger child or an adult, add squares to the back and subtract from the front. The sleeves can be lengthened by adding squares.

Spinning Notes

Fiber: 12 oz (340 g) Bluefaced Leicester handpainted top.

Shown here: Chameleon Colorworks BFL, "October" colorway.

Preparation: Divide top in half, split each piece lengthwise into fourths, and predraft each section.

Drafting method: Semiwoolen.

Wheel system: Scotch tension.

Ratio (singles/plying): 6:1/10:1.

Singles direction spun: Z.

Number of plies: 2.

Plied direction spun: S.

Plied twists per inch: 4.

Plied wraps per inch: 14.

Total yardage: 737 yd (674 m).

Yards per pound: 983.

Knitting Notes

Yarn classification: DK weight (Light #3).

Yardage used: 719 yd (657 m).

Needles: U.S. size 2 (2.75 mm)—Straight and double-pointed (dpn). Adjust needle size if necessary to obtain the correct gauge.

Gauge: 24 sts and 43 rows = 4" (10 cm) in garter st; each mitered square measures 1¾" (4.5 cm) wide and 1¾" (4.5 cm) long.

Notions: Five ⅝" (1.6 cm) buttons; tapestry needle; stitch markers.

Finished size: 22½" (57 cm) finished chest, buttoned, and including 1½" (3.8 cm) front bands. To fit child's 24 months to 3T.

Note: Size can be adjusted by changing the size of the mitered square; every ¼" (6 mm) added or removed from the size of the square will increase or decrease the finished chest by about 3" (7.5 cm) and lengthen or shorten the body by about 2" (5 cm) and the sleeves by 1" (2.5 cm).

stitch guide Mitered Square

Beg with 20 sts, either CO, picked up, or a combination of both as given in directions.

ROW 1: (RS) K8, k2tog, place marker (pm), k2tog, k8—18 sts rem.

EVEN-NUMBERED ROWS 2-16: Knit.

ROW 3: K7, k2tog, ssk, k7—16 sts rem.

ROW 5: K6, k2tog, ssk, k6—14 sts rem.

ROWS 7-15: Continue as established, working one fewer st before and after decs on each RS row—4 sts rem.

ROW 17: K2tog, ssk—2 sts rem.

ROW 18: (WS) Knit.

ROW 19: K2tog—1 st rem. Continue according to directions.

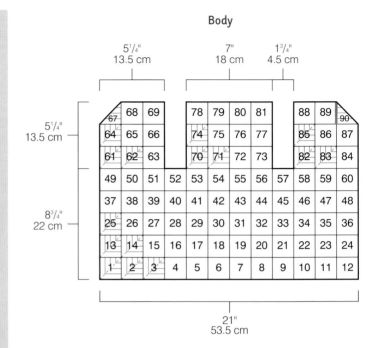

Body

LOWER BODY

Square 1

CO 20 sts loosely using the backward-loop method (see Glossary), and work mitered square (see Stitch Guide) for Square 1—1 st rem; do not break yarn.

Square 2

With WS of Square 1 facing, pick up and purl (see Glossary) 9 sts along selvedge of Square 1, pm, then use backward-loop method to CO 10 sts for a total of 20 sts, and work mitered square—1 st rem; do not break yarn.

Squares 3–12

Following Body diagram, work as for Square 2, picking up first 9 sts of each square along WS of previous square. The angle of the miters and direction of garter ridges are shown on selected squares on diagrams to help you orient the squares correctly. Break yarn after Square 12 and draw through rem st.

Square 13

With WS facing, use backward-loop method to CO 10 sts, pm, pick up and purl 10 sts from upper edge of Square 1 for a total of 20 sts, and work mitered square—1 st rem.

Square 14

With WS facing, pick up and purl 9 sts along selvedge of Square 13, pm, pick up and purl 10 sts along top edge of Square 2 for a total of 20 sts, and work mitered square—1 st rem.

Squares 15–60

Following Body diagram, continue squares as established—piece measures about 8¾" (22 cm) from lower edge and 21" (53.5 cm) wide. Break yarn after Square 60 and draw through rem st.

LEFT FRONT

Squares 61–66

Work Squares 61–66 according to diagram, then break yarn after Square 66 and draw through rem st.

Triangle 67

Rejoin yarn with WS facing to outer corner of Square 64 and pick up and purl 10 sts across top edge of Square 64.

ROW 1: (RS) K8, k2tog—9 sts rem.

EVEN-NUMBERED ROWS 2–16: Knit.

ROW 3: K7, k2tog—8 sts rem.

ROWS 5–15: Continue as established, working one fewer st before dec on each RS row—2 sts rem.

ROW 17: K2tog—1 st rem. Break yarn and fasten off rem st.

Squares 68 and 69

Work according to diagram, picking up 9 sts along selvedge of Triangle 67 for Square 68. Break yarn after Square 69 and draw through rem st.

55

Back

8³/₄"
22 cm

5¹/₄"
13.5 cm

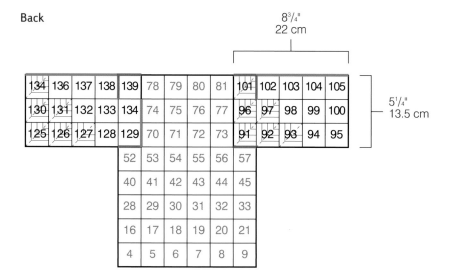

134	136	137	138	139	78	79	80	81	101	102	103	104	105
130	131	132	133	134	74	75	76	77	96	97	98	99	100
125	126	127	128	129	70	71	72	73	91	92	93	94	95

52	53	54	55	56	57
40	41	42	43	44	45
28	29	30	31	32	33
16	17	18	19	20	21
4	5	6	7	8	9

Front

8³/₄"
22 cm

3¹/₂"
9 cm

		121	122				155	156					
116	117	118	119	120	88	89	90	67	68	69	150	151	152	153	154
111	112	113	114	115	85	86	87	64	65	66	145	146	147	148	149
106	107	108	109	110	82	83	84	61	62	63	140	141	142	143	144

58	59	60	49	50	51
46	47	48	37	38	39
34	35	36	25	26	27
22	23	24	13	14	15
10	11	12	1	2	3

BACK

Squares 70–81

Work according to diagram. Break yarn after Square 81 and draw through rem st.

RIGHT FRONT

Squares 82–89

Work according to diagram. Break yarn after Square 89 and draw through rem st.

Triangle 90

Rejoin yarn with WS facing to inner corner where Squares 86, 87, and 89 meet. Pick up and purl 10 sts along top edge of Square 87.

ROW 1: (RS) K2tog, k8—9 sts rem.
EVEN-NUMBERED ROWS 2–16: Knit.
ROW 3: K2tog, k7—8 sts rem.
ODD-NUMBERED ROWS 5–15: Continue as established, working one fewer st after dec on each RS row—2 sts rem.
ROW 17: K2tog—1 st rem.
Break yarn, leaving a tail long enough for sewing, and fasten off rem st. Use yarn tail threaded on a tapestry needle to sew short seam between Square 89 and Triangle 90 indicated by green line on diagram.

SLEEVES

For each sleeve, work the squares of the back, then the front. Make sure to note where the squares are not joined (red lines on diagrams) because the underarm and shoulder gussets will be inserted between squares at those locations.

Right Back Sleeve

Work Squares 91–101 according to Back diagram, casting on for bottom of Square 91 so it is not joined to the top of Square 57, and casting on for the side of Square

102 so it is not joined to Square 101. Break yarn after Square 105 and draw through rem st.

Right Front Sleeve

Work Squares 106–120 according to Front diagram. The lower edges of Squares 106–109 are picked up from the lower edges of Squares 92–95 of right back sleeve. CO the lower edge of Square 110 so it is not joined to Square 91. Break yarn after Square 120 and draw through rem st. Sew sides of Squares 110, 115, and 120 to body Squares 82, 85, and 88 as shown by green line. Sew back and front sleeves tog along upper edges as shown by green line, leaving Squares 101 and 120 unjoined.

Right Shoulder Saddle

Work Squares 121 and 122 according to Front diagram. Break yarn after Square 122 and draw through rem st. For shoulder seam, sew the top edges of Squares 121 and 101 tog, then sew the top edges of Squares 122 and 81 tog. This will leave a square opening at the shoulder bounded on its four sides by Squares 101, 102, 120, and 121 for shoulder gusset.

Right Shoulder Gusset

For shoulder gusset Square 123 (not shown on diagrams), with WS facing, pick up and purl 10 sts along Square 101, pm, then pick up and purl 10 sts along Square 102—20 sts. Continue as foll:

ROW 1: (RS) K8, k2tog, sl m, k2tog, k7, sl last st temporarily to right needle, lift a loop from garter ridge of Square 121 selvedge onto right needle, return last st and lifted loop to left needle and knit

them tog to join end of row to Square 121—2 sts dec'd from gusset square.

ROW 2: (WS) Knit to last st, sl last st to right needle, lift a loop from garter ridge of Square 120 selvedge onto right needle, return last st and lifted loop to left needle and knit them tog to join end of row to Square 120—no change to gusset square st count.

ROWS 3–16: Rep Rows 1 and 2 seven more times—4 gusset square sts rem.

ROW 17: K2tog, sl last 2 sts temporarily to right needle, lift a loop from garter ridge of Square 121 selvedge onto right needle, return last 2 sts and lifted loop to left needle and work them tog as sssk (see Glossary)—2 gusset square sts rem.

ROW 18: (WS) K1, sl last st to right needle, lift a loop from garter ridge of Square 120 selvedge onto right needle, return last st and lifted loop to left needle and work them as k2tog.

ROW 19: K2tog—1 gusset square st rem. Break yarn and draw through rem st.

57

Right Underarm Gusset

There will be a triangular opening at the underarm bounded on its three sides by Squares 57, 91, and 110. For underarm gusset Triangle 124 (not shown on diagrams), with WS facing, pick up and purl 10 sts along the rem side of Square 110, pm, then pick up and purl 10 sts along rem side of Square 91—20 sts. Sl a third dpn into 10 garter selvedge loops along edge of Square 57; these sts are just placed on the needle, not picked up and purled. Continue for Triangle 124 as foll:

ROW 1: (RS) K2tog, k6, k2tog, sl m, k2tog, k6, knit last 2 sts tog with 1 st from end of Square 57 needle—4 sts dec'd from gusset triangle; 1 st joined from third needle.

ROW 2: (WS) Knit to last st, knit last st tog with 1 st from other end of Square 57 needle tog to join end of row to Square 120—no change to gusset triangle st count; 1 st joined from third needle.

ROWS 3–8: Rep Rows 1 and 2 three more times—4 gusset triangle sts rem; 2 sts on third needle.

ROW 9: K2tog, work last 2 sts and 1 st from third needle as sssk—2 gusset triangle sts and 1 st on third needle.

ROW 10: K1, knit last st tog with rem st on third needle—2 gusset triangle sts rem.

ROW 11: K2tog—1 gusset square st rem. Break yarn and draw through rem st.

Left Back Sleeve

Work Squares 125–139 according to Back diagram, casting on for bottom of Square 129 so it is not joined to the top of Square 52, and casting on for the side of Square 139 so it is not joined to Square 138. Break yarn after Square 139, and draw through rem st. Sew sides of Squares 129 and 134 to body Squares 70 and 74 as shown by green line.

Left Front Sleeve

Work Squares 140–154 according to Front diagram. The lower edges of Squares 141–144 are picked up from the lower edges of Squares 125–128 of left back sleeve. CO the lower edge of Square 140 so it is not joined to Square 129. Break

yarn after Square 154 and draw through rem st. Sew back and front sleeves tog along upper edges as shown by green line, leaving Squares 139 and 150 unjoined.

Left Shoulder Saddle

Work Squares 155 and 156 according to Front diagram. Break yarn after Square 156 and draw through rem st. For shoulder seam, sew the top edges of Squares 155 and 78 tog, then sew the top edges of Squares 156 and 139 tog. This will leave a square opening at the shoulder bounded on its four sides by Squares 138, 139, 150, and 156 for shoulder gusset.

Left Shoulder Gusset

For shoulder gusset Square 157 (not shown on diagrams), with WS facing, pick up and purl 10 sts along Square 138, pm, then pick up and purl 10 sts along Square 139—20 sts. Continue as foll:

ROW 1: (RS) K8, k2tog, sl m, k2tog, k7, sl last st temporarily to right needle, lift a loop from garter ridge of Square 150 selvedge onto right needle, return last st and lifted loop to left needle and knit them tog to join end of row to Square 150—2 sts dec'd from gusset square.

ROW 2: (WS) Knit to last st, sl last st to right needle, lift a loop from garter ridge of Square 156 selvedge onto right needle, return last st and lifted loop to left needle and knit them tog to join end of row to Square 156—no change to gusset square st count.

ROWS 3–19: Work as for right shoulder gusset, continuing to join to Squares 150 and 156.

Break yarn and draw through rem st.

Left Underarm Gusset

There will be a triangular opening at the underarm bounded on its three sides by Squares 52, 129, and 140. For underarm gusset Triangle 158 (not shown on diagrams), with WS facing, pick up and purl 10 sts along the rem side of Square 129, pm, then pick up and purl 10 sts along rem side of Square 140—20 sts. Sl a third dpn into 10 garter selvedge loops along edge of Square 52; these sts are just placed on the needle, not picked up and purled.

Work Rows 1–11 as for right underarm gusset. Break yarn and draw through rem st.

FINISHING

Front Bands

Note: Buttonholes are on left front as is customary for boys' or unisex garments. With WS facing and beg at right neck edge where Square 87 and Triangle 90 meet, pick up and purl 70 sts along right front (10 sts per square). Knit 18 rows, ending with a WS row—9 garter ridges completed. BO all sts kwise. With WS facing and beg at lower edge of left front, pick up and purl 70 sts along left front (10 sts per square)

to end where Square 64 and Triangle 67 meet. Knit 10 rows, ending with a WS row.

NEXT ROW: (RS, buttonhole row) K5, *BO 4 sts, knit until there are 10 sts on needle after BO gap; rep from * three more times, BO 4 sts, knit to end.

NEXT ROW: (WS) Knit, using the backward-loop method to CO 4 sts over each gap in previous row to complete buttonholes. Knit 6 more rows, then BO all sts kwise.

Collar

With RS facing and beg where Square 87 and Triangle 90 meet, pick up and knit 55 sts evenly spaced around neck edge, ending where Square 64 and Triangle 67 meet (about 9 sts for each square or triangle in neck edge). Knit 3 rows, beg and ending with a WS row.

NEXT ROW: (RS) *K11, M1 (see Glossary); rep from * to end—60 sts. *Note:* RS of collar corresponds to WS of garment, so RS of collar will show on the outside when the collar is folded back.

Work short-rows (see Glossary) to shape individual collar triangles as foll:

SHORT-ROW 1: (RS of collar, WS of garment) K2, turn.

EVEN-NUMBERED SHORT-ROWS 2–18: (WS of collar) Sl 1 as if to purl with yarn in front (pwise wyf), knit to end.

SHORT-ROW 3: K3, turn.

SHORT-ROWS 4–18: Continue as established, knitting one more st every RS row before turning; Short-row 18 should be worked as sl 1, k9.

SHORT-ROW 19: Sl 1, *k1, BO 1 st; rep from * to last st of triangle, knit next live st, BO final triangle st, k1—2 sts on right needle for start of next triangle (counts as first RS row of next triangle).

Rep Short-rows 2–19 (do not rep Row 1) five more times, BO to end on Short-row 19 of last triangle. Break yarn and draw through rem st. Weave in ends.

Handwash sweater in warm water with wool-safe detergent, lay flat to dry with towels inside to maintain shape, and fold collar triangles to the outside as shown. Sew on buttons and convince your toddler that she really wants to wear her lovely new sweater.

stained glass cap and mittens

{Carol Huebscher Rhoades}

This elegant winter set was inspired by Danish designs that include garter-stitch "buds" framed by garter and slipped stitches in a contrasting thinner yarn. A very fine kid mohair/silk yarn provides a delicate edge framing the sportweight angora/wool blend "buds." To create a yarn that would shift colors gently, Carol Rhoades made a two-ply yarn using two sets of 12-inch color segments of space-dyed roving for the hat and two sets of 4½-inch color segments for each mitten. The occasional color overlap in plying helped the yarn blend smoothly from one color to the next.

Spinning Notes

Fiber: 5 oz solid and space-dyed yarns—50% Polwarth wool/50% kid mohair roving; laceweight—¾ oz kid mohair/silk rolags.

Shown here: Polwarth/mohair blend—hand-painted roving from Rovings; Texas kid mohair from Kai Ranch and Bombyx mori silk from The Fold, handcarded.

Preparation: Sportweight—commercial prepared roving; laceweight—rolags.

Drafting method: Sportweight—short backward draw; laceweight—long draw.

Wheel system: Double drive.

Ratio (singles/plying): Sportweight—9:1/11:1; laceweight—13:1/15:1.

Singles direction spun: Z.

Singles twists per inch: Sportweight—9.

Singles wraps per inch: Sportweight—20; laceweight—50.

Number of plies: 2.

Plied direction spun: S.

Plied twists per inch: Sportweight—6; laceweight—13.

Plied wraps per inch: Sportweight—15; laceweight—36.

Total yardage: Sportweight—black, 240 yd (219 m); multicolor, 72 yd (66 m) for cap and 39 yd (36 m) for mittens; laceweight—177 yd (162 m).

Yards per pound: Sportweight—1,135; laceweight—4,380.

Knitting Notes

Yarn classification: Sportweight (Fine #2) and laceweight (Lace #0).

Yardage used: Cap—black sportweight, 90 yd (82 m); multicolor sportweight, 32 yd (29 m); white laceweight, 61 yd (56 m). Mittens—black sportweight, 150 yd (137 m); multicolor sportweight, 22 yd (20 m); white laceweight, 30 yd (27 m).

Needles: U.S. sizes 2 (2.75 mm) and 1½ (2.5 mm): set of 5 double-pointed (dpn) and 24" (60 cm) circular (cir). Adjust needle sizes if necessary to obtain the correct gauge.

Notions: Stitch holder; stitch marker (m); tapestry needle.

Gauge: 28 sts and 40 rnds = 4" (10 cm) in St st on smaller needles; 15 sts and 17 rnds = 2" (5 cm) in chain net pattern.

Finished size: Cap—about 20½" (52 cm) circumference and 8¼" (21 cm) tall. Mittens—8" (20.5 cm) hand circumference and 11" (28 cm) from cuff to top. To fit a women's medium.

61

stitch guide Chain Net pattern

(multiple of 2 sts)
RND 1: With white, knit.
RND 2: With white, purl.
RND 3: With multicolor, *sl 1 wyb, k1; rep from * to end.
RND 4: With multicolor, *sl 1 wyb, p1; rep from * to end.
Rep Rnds 1–4 for patt, carrying unused colors between rnds.

CAP

Rolled Brim
With black and larger cir, CO 144 sts. Place marker (pm) and join for working in the rnd, being careful not to twist sts. Knit 6 rnds.

Window Pattern
Work Rnds 1–4 of Chain Net pattern twelve times, then rep Rnds 1 and 2 once more.

Body
With black and smaller cir, work in St st for 1¾" (4.5 cm) or to desired length to crown (about 18 rounds).

Crown Shaping
Note: Change to dpns when sts become too tight to work on cir needle.
RND 1: *K16, k2tog; rep from * to end.
RND 2 AND ALL EVEN-NUMBERED RNDS: Knit.
RND 3: *K15, k2tog; rep from * to end. Continue to decrease as established, working 1 fewer st between decs on each dec rnd, fourteen more times—16 sts rem.
NEXT RND: Knit.
NEXT RND: [K2tog] to end—8 sts rem. Cut yarn, draw tail through rem sts, and fasten off inside.

RIGHT MITTEN
With black and larger dpns, CO 57 sts. Join for working in the rnd as foll: pass last CO st over first CO st (1 st dec'd) and return first st to left needle—56 sts rem. Knit 6 rnds.

Window Pattern
Work Rnds 1–4 of Chain Net pattern twelve times, then rep Rnds 1 and 2 once more.

Hand
With black and smaller dpns, knit 6 rnds.

Thumb Gusset

RND 1: (inc rnd) Work right-slanting lifted increase (see Glossary), k3, work left-slanting lifted increase (see Glossary), pm, knit to end—58 sts.

RNDS 2–4: Knit.

RND 5: (inc rnd) Work right-slanting lifted increase, knit to m, work left-slanting lifted increase (before m), knit to end—2 sts inc'd.

RNDS 6–8: Knit.

Rep Rnds 5–8 three more times, then rep Rnds 5 and 6 once more—15 sts between m, 68 sts total.

NEXT RND: Place 15 gusset sts on hold for thumb, CO 3 sts over gap, knit to end—56 sts.

Knit 34 rnds or to desired length to tip of little finger.

Top Shaping

NEXT RND: (dec rnd) *K1, ssk, k22, k2tog, k1; rep from * to end—52 sts rem.

NEXT RND: (dec rnd) *K1, ssk, k20, k2tog, k1; rep from * to end—4 sts dec'd.

Rep dec rnd, working 2 fewer sts between decs on each rnd, ten more times—8 sts rem. Arrange sts for front of hand on one dpn and back of hand on another dpn. Graft using the Kitchener st (see Glossary).

Thumb

With smaller dpns and black, k15 held thumb gusset sts, pick up and knit (see Glossary) 5 sts across gap—20 sts.

Knit 20 rnds or to middle of thumbnail.

RND 21: *K2, k2tog; rep from * to end—15 sts rem.

RNDS 22 AND 24: Knit.

RND 23: *K1, k2tog; rep from * to end—10 sts rem.

RND 25: [K2tog] to end—5 sts rem.

Cut yarn, draw tail through rem sts, and fasten off inside. Weave in all ends.

LEFT MITTEN

Work as for right mitten to thumb gusset.

Thumb gusset

RND 1: (inc rnd) K25, pm, work right-slanting lifted increase (see Glossary), k3, work left-slanting lifted increase (see Glossary), pm, knit to end—58 sts.

RNDS 2–4: Knit.

RND 5: (inc rnd) K25, work right-slanting lifted increase, knit to m, work left-slanting lifted increase (before m), knit to end—2 sts inc'd.

RNDS 6–8: Knit.

Rep Rnds 5–8 three more times, then rep Rnds 5 and 6 once more—15 sts between m, 68 sts total.

NEXT RND: K25, place 15 gusset sts on hold for thumb, CO 3 sts over gap, knit to end—56 sts.

Knit 34 rnds or to desired length to tip of little finger.

Work as for right mitten to end.

FINISHING

Weave in all ends on WS except for tail from CO; as cuff will roll outward, weave in tail on RS to first rnd of white, then fasten off on WS.

nomad bag

{Sara Lamb}

Inspired by traditional rugs and textiles of the Imazighen, or Berber tribes of the Atlas Mountains, this bag is knitted of sturdy three-ply yarns spun from longwool breeds of Romney, Lincoln, Karakul, and mohair. The red, gold, black, and white colors are found in many tribal and nomadic cultures that relied for centuries on the natural colors of sheep and goat wool and natural dyes of madder roots and chamomile flowers. Sara Lamb embellished the bag with coins and talismans for good luck.

Spinning Notes

Fiber: 17 oz (482 g) longwool roving.

Shown here: 8 oz (227 g) Lincoln/mohair (dyed red), 3 oz (85 g) black Karakul, and 12 oz (170 g) Romney/gray mohair (half dyed yellow) pin-drafted rovings from Morro Fleece Works.

Drafting method: Long draw.

Wheel system: Scotch tension.

Ratio (singles/plying): 17:1 (singles).

Singles direction spun: Z.

Number of plies: 3.

Plied direction spun: S.

Plied twists per inch: Red—4; yellow—3; white—3; black—4.

Plied wraps per inch: Red—15; yellow—14; white—14; black—11.

Total yardage: Red—175 yd (160 m); yellow—84 yd (77 m); white—84 yd (77 m); black—61 yd (56 m).

Yards per pound: Red—350; yellow—450; white—450; black—325.

Knitting Notes

Yarn classification: DK weight (Light #3).

Yardage used: Red—135 yd (123 m); yellow—51 yd (47 m); white—51 yd (47 m); black—27 yd (25 m).

Needles: U.S. size 3 (3.25 mm): straight. U.S. size 2 (2.75 mm): set of 5 double-pointed (dpn). Adjust needle sizes if necessary to obtain the correct gauge.

Notions: Tapestry needle; sewing machine; iron; scissors.

Materials: 4"×20" (10×51 cm) ultrasuede for binding; 20"×24" (51×61 cm) iron-on interfacing; 20"×24" (51×61 cm) silk ikat fabric for lining; silk cord for closing loop; matching thread; buttons, glass beads, charms, and old coins for embellishment.

Gauge: 10 sts and 12 rows = 2" (5 cm) in St st before finishing.

Finished size: 8½" (21.5 cm) wide, 10" (25.5 cm) tall, and 2" (5 cm) deep, with 32" (81.5 cm) strap.

Note: Carry unused colors up along the edge of the knitting if there are only a few rows before they will be used again, twisting yarns to secure floats.

Front

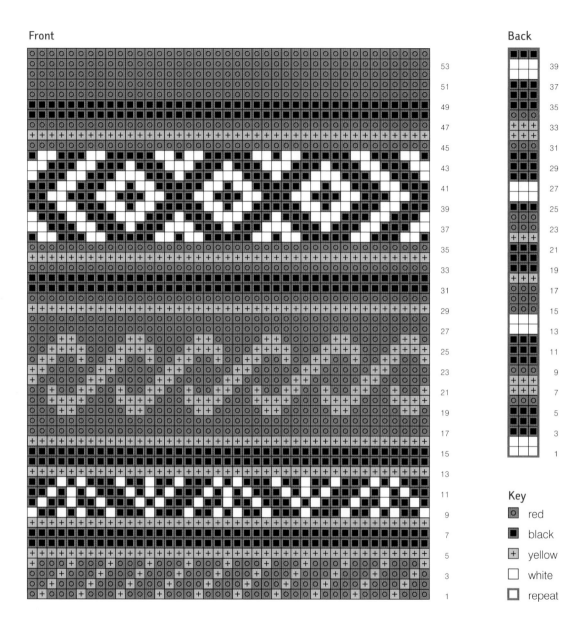

53
51
49
47
45
43
41
39
37
35
33
31
29
27
25
23
21
19
17
15
13
11
9
7
5
3
1

Back

39
37
35
33
31
29
27
25
23
21
19
17
15
13
11
9
7
5
3
1

Key

⊙	red
■	black
+	yellow
□	white
□	repeat

1a

1b

BAG

Body Panel

With red and larger needles, CO 41 sts.
  Work 3 rows in St st.
  Work Rows 1–40 of Back chart.
  With red, work 23 rows in St st.
  Work Rows 1–54 of Front chart.
  BO all sts. Weave in ends and block flat.
  To strengthen the knitted fabric and prevent stretching, iron interfacing (following manufacturer's instructions) to WS of bag. Finish the CO and BO ends of the bag as foll: Cut the ultrasuede into two 4" x 10" (10 x 25.5 cm) pieces. *Lay the knitted panel face up and center one piece of ultrasuede over the CO end with WS facing up. Align the top edges of the bag and ultrasuede. With sewing thread and sewing machine or sewing needle, sew both layers together (**Figure 1a**). Fold the ultrasuede up, then wrap the excess along the sides of the bag to the back. Fold the top edge of the ultrasuede over to the back of the bag. Sew through both layers just below the front edge of the ultrasuede (**Figure 1b**). Repeat from * for the other end.

Handle

With red and dpns, CO 20 sts. Join for working in the rnd, being careful not to twist sts.
  Knit for desired length and work band patt along strap as desired (see page 68 for Handle chart); strap is attached from bottom of bag. BO sts and block flat.

67

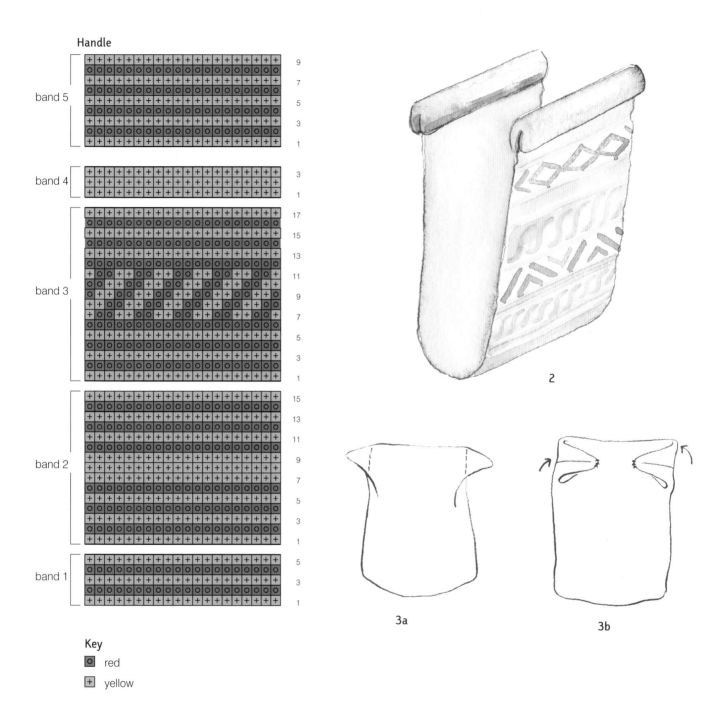

Handle

band 5

band 4

band 3

band 2

band 1

Key

⊙ red

+ yellow

2

3a

3b

FINISHING

Stitch four rows the full length of the band (two rows on each edge) to strengthen and stabilize it.

Fold the bag in half so that the interfacing is on the interior and the CO and BO edges are held together (**Figure 2**). Use pins to mark the fold at the bottom of the bag along each edge. With WS of bag and handle facing up, place the one end of the handle perpendicular to the bag so that the center of the band abuts the marked fold of the bag. *With a sewing needle and thread, use invisible seam (see Glossary) to join the bottom of the band to the bag, then use mattress stitch (see Glossary) to join the side of the band to the side of the bag. Repeat to sew the other side of the band to the other side of the bag. Position the other end of the bag abutting the center of the other side of the bag, being careful not to twist the strap, and repeat from * for the second side.

Lining

Cut lining fabric to dimensions of bag plus 1" (2.5 cm) seam allowance. Sew side seams. Miter lower corners as foll: Fold the bottom corners of the lining out 1" (2.5 cm) and sew across the corners (**Figure 3a**). Fold the corners to the bottom of the bag and stitch them in place (**Figure 3b**).

With WS of lining facing, insert in bag. Fold under top edges of lining so top of lining meets seam in ultrasuede and stitch in place. Sew button below ultrasuede centered on front of bag. Make a twisted cord (see Glossary) and sew to back of bag for closure. Embellish as desired and enjoy!

diamonds and pearls lace mitts

{Emma Crew}

These elegant mitts were inspired by a pair of wonderfully warm but utilitarian garter-stitch handwarmers made in a class. Wanting something a little dressier, Emma Crew designed a pair that included lace and a thumb, then accented the garter lace with glistening beads. This project is ideal for showcasing a small amount of really luxurious fiber in an elegant and useful item. They knit up fairly quickly and make a wonderful gift, but be warned: everyone who tries them on will want a pair!

Spinning Notes

Fiber: 1½ oz (43 g) 34% superfine Merino/33% cashmere/33% silk batt.

Shown here: Franquemont Fibers luxury batt.

Drafting method: Long draw.

Spindle: Top whorl.

Singles direction spun: Z.

Number of plies: 2.

Plied direction spun: S.

Plied wraps per inch: 18 before washing; 16 after washing.

Plied twists per inch: 5.5.

Total yardage: 180 yd (165 m).

Yards per pound: About 1,920.

Knitting Notes

Yarn classification: Sportweight (Fine #2).

Yardage used: 160 yd (146 m).

Needles: U.S. size 3 (3.25 mm): straight. Adjust needle size if necessary to obtain the correct gauge.

Gauge: 25 sts and 56 rows = 4" (10 cm) in garter st.

Finished size: About 7" (18 cm) hand circumference and about 7½" (19 cm) from upper edge to deepest point; to fit an average woman's hand.

Notions: Markers (m); 160 3mm cylinder beads; small crochet hook in size to fit through beads; tapestry needle.

stitch guide

Wrap and Turn On WS rows, work in patt to wrapped st symbol (1 st before marker), sl st to be wrapped as if to purl with yarn in back (pwise wyb), turn work so RS is facing, take yarn to the back between needles, return wrapped st to right needle, and cont in patt for next RS row of chart. Work the wrapped st tog with its wrap when you next come to it.

Place Bead Begin each beaded st by sliding a bead onto crochet hook. For beads in the middle of the work, work in patt to the bead symbol, knit the st to be beaded, hook the top of the st just worked and remove it temporarily from the needle (Figure 1), slide the bead down the hook and onto the st (Figure 2), then return the st to the right needle (Figure 3). For beads at the end of RS rows (lace edge), work in patt to the last st, hook the yo of the previous WS row, slide the bead down the hook and onto the yo, return the yo to the left needle, then knit the yo.

Figure 1   Figure 2   Figure 3

Grafting in Garter Stitch With sts evenly distributed on 2 needles, hold needles so that the yarn comes off of the lower needle on the right-hand side. The lower needle should have the purl bumps closest to the needle on the side facing the knitter, while the purl bumps closest to the needle are facing away from you on the upper needle. Insert tapestry needle through first st on upper needle as if to purl, leaving st on needle. *Insert tapestry needle into first st on lower needle as if to knit, remove st. Insert tapestry needle into next st on lower needle as if to purl; leave st on needle. Repeat from *on upper needle. Continue alternating lower and upper needles to end of row. (It may help to think to yourself, "First st as if to knit and off, next st as if to purl and on.")

MITTS
Right Hand
Using a provisional method (see Glossary), CO 45 sts. Knit 1 WS row. Rep Rows 1–12 of Lace Mitt chart six times, placing marker (pm) after first 24 sts as shown on chart. *Note:* To adjust hand circumference, work more or fewer 12-row reps here; every 12 rows added or removed will increase or reduce the hand circumference by about ½" (1.3 cm). (See suggestions on page 73 for additional customizing tips.) Work Rows 13–72 of chart, then work Rows 1–9 once more.

right thumb
Work short-rows over 15 outlined thumb sts to shape thumb as foll; these short-rows are not shown on chart:
SHORT-ROW 1: (WS, Row 10 of chart) Work in patt to m, sl m, k1, knit the 15 outlined sts, turn without wrapping last st (selvedge of thumb opening).
SHORT-ROW 2: (RS) K14, wrap next st, turn.
SHORT-ROW 3: K13, sl 1 pwise with yarn in front (wyf; thumb opening selvedge st). For rem short-rows, sl the thumb opening selvedge st pwise with yarn in front (wyf) at end of WS short-rows, and knit it at beg of RS short-rows.
SHORT-ROW 4: K13, wrap next st, turn.
SHORT-ROW 5: K12, sl 1.
SHORT-ROW 6: Knit to 1 st before previously wrapped st, wrap next st, turn.
SHORT-ROW 7: Knit to last thumb st, sl 1.
SHORT-ROWS 8–25: Rep Short-rows 6 and 7 nine more times; Short-row 25 should have been worked as k2, sl 1.
SHORT-ROW 26: K2, wrap next st, turn.
SHORT-ROW 27: K1, temporarily sl next st to right needle, with left needle tip, lift the purl bump of the thumb opening selvedge st from Short-row 1 onto the left

needle, return the slipped st to the left needle, k2tog (slipped st and lifted bump loop tog), work to end of needle as k7, sl 1; this completes Row 10 of chart. Work Row 11 of chart across all sts, working wrapped thumb sts tog with their wraps as you come to them, and ending with a RS row—45 sts rem (21 sts in lace cuff section and 24 sts in hand section). Piece measures about 7" (18 cm) from CO along selvedge at upper edge of hand; 12 lace points completed at cuff edge. Break yarn, leaving about a 1 yd (1 m) tail.

Remove provisional CO, place live sts from provisional cast-on onto spare needle, and use garter method (see Stitch Guide) to graft sts tog.

Left Hand
Using a provisional method, CO 45 sts. Knit 1 WS row. Work Rows 1–5 of Lace Mitt chart, pm after first 24 sts as shown on chart.

 Sizing Options

For different hand sizes, work more or fewer repeats as indicated in the instructions. The fabric should be slightly snug around the wrist (above the short-row turning points), and the garter stitch hand section should stretch to accommodate a range of sizes. If the wrist fits well but the palm is still too small, add a gusset before working the last RS chart row as foll:

Short-row 1: (RS) K5, wrap next st, turn.
Short-row 2: (WS) K4, sl last st pwise wyf.
Short-row 3: Knit to previously wrapped st, work wrapped st tog with its wrap, k5, wrap next st, turn.
Short-row 4: Knit to last st, sl 1.
Short-rows 5–8: Rep Short-rows 3 and 4 two times; Short-row 8 should have been worked as k22, sl 1; last wrapped st is 24th st from upper edge.
Work last row(s) of chart as given in the instructions, then graft ends tog.

The thumbs shown are worked over 15 stitches and 26 rows (13 garter ridges). To adjust the size of the thumb opening, wrap part of the already-completed garter st hand section around your thumb and count the number of garter ridges that fit comfortably. Add 2 to the number of ridges that fit around your thumb and work the thumb shaping using that number of stitches, adjusting the instructions to fit your stitch count. For example, if you need 15 garter ridges instead of 13 ridges to fit around your thumb, work the thumb short-rows over 17 stitches. Work right thumb Short-row 2 as k16, wrap next st, turn; and continue working left thumb short-rows until you have completed a RS row worked as k16, wrap next st, turn. In this example, for both thumbs the last wrapped stitch should be the seventeenth stitch from the thumb opening selvedge.

73

Lace Mitt

Key

- k on RS; p on WS
- · p on RS; k on WS
- O yo
- ╱ k2tog on both RS and WS
- ╲ ssk
- ⋀ sl 2 as if to k2tog, k1, p2sso
- V sl 1 pwise wyf on WS
- W wrap st and turn (see Stitch Guide)
- B place bead (see Stitch Guide)
- no stitch
- pattern repeat
- | marker position
- thumb placement

71
69
67
65
63
61
59
57
55
53
51
49
47
45
43
41
39
37
35
33
31
29
27
25
23
21
19
17
15
13
11
9
7
5
3
1

74

left thumb

Work short-rows over 15 outlined thumb sts to shape thumb as foll:

SHORT-ROW 1: (WS, Row 6 of chart) Work in patt to m, sl m, k1, knit the 15 outlined sts, turn without wrapping last st (selvedge of thumb opening).

SHORT-ROW 2: (RS) K2, wrap next st, turn.

SHORT-ROW 3: K1, sl 1 pwise wyf (thumb opening selvedge st).

SHORT-ROW 4: K2, work wrapped st tog with its wrap, wrap next st, turn.

SHORT-ROW 5: K2, sl 1.

SHORT-ROW 6: Knit to previously wrapped st, work wrap st tog with its wrap, wrap next st, turn.

SHORT-ROW 7: Knit to last thumb st, sl 1.

SHORT-ROWS 8–25: Rep Short-rows 6 and 7 nine more times; Short-row 25 should have been worked as k12, sl 1.

SHORT-ROW 26: K13, work wrapped st tog with its wrap, wrap next st, turn.

SHORT-ROW 27: Knit to last thumb st, temporarily sl next st to right needle, with left needle tip, lift the purl bump of the thumb opening selvedge st from Short-row 1 onto the left needle, return the slipped st to the left needle, k2tog (slipped st and lifted bump loop tog), work to end of needle as k7, sl 1; this completes Row 6 of chart.

NEXT ROW: (RS) Work Row 7 of chart across all sts, working rem wrapped st tog with its wrap as you come to it. Work Rows 8–72 of chart once, rep Rows 1–12 five times, then work Rows 1–11 once more, ending with a RS row—45 sts rem (21 sts in lace cuff section and 24 sts in hand section). Piece measures about 7" (18 cm) from CO along selvedge at upper edge of hand; 12 lace points completed at cuff edge.

Break yarn and graft ends of mitt tog as for right hand.

FINISHING

Weave in ends. Wash and block, pinning out points of lace cuffs, and coaxing garter ridges in hand section close together to maintain elasticity.

spider hat

{Nancy Roberts}

A trip to Peru, where Nancy Roberts saw traditional Peruvian weaving patterns depicting spiders, or *arañas*, inspired this hat design. This handspun and handknitted version is a tribute to the original spinners. Nancy created the long repeats of color in the variegated yarn by machine knitting the handspun yarn and dyeing the knitted fabric. She frogged (ripped) the dyed blank and knitted it in the two-color pattern with the black yarn.

Spinning Notes

Fiber: 4 oz variegated yarn (MC): Polwarth; 3 oz black yarn (B): 50% Polwarth/50% kid mohair.

Preparation: Commercially carded roving.

Drafting method: Long draw.

Wheel system: Scotch tension.

Ratio (singles/plying): 15.5:1.

Singles direction spun: Z.

Singles twists per inch: 7.

Singles wraps per inch: 22.

Twist angle: 25°.

Number of plies: 2.

Plied direction spun: S.

Plied twists per inch: 10.5.

Plied wraps per inch: 16.

Total yardage: 375 yd (343 m) MC and 280 yd (256 m) B.

Yards per pound: 1,700.

Knitting Notes

Yarn classification: Fingering (Super Fine #1).

Yardage used: 375 yd (343 m) MC and 280 yd (256 m) B.

Needles: U.S. size 1 (2.25 mm): 16" (40 cm) circular (cir) and set of 5 double-pointed (dpn). U.S. size 2 (2.75 mm): 16" (40 cm) cir. Adjust needle sizes if necessary to obtain the correct gauge.

Notions: Crochet hook; waste yarn; stitch marker (m); tapestry needle.

Gauge: 14½ sts and 17 rnds = 2" (5 cm).

Finished size: 20" (51 cm) circumference and 9¼" (24 cm) from hem to top. To fit a woman's size medium/large.

Key

- ◆ B
- ☐ MC
- ☐ pattern repeat

Spider

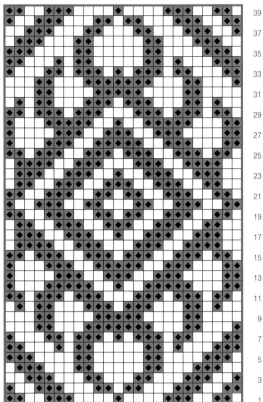

HEM

Using crochet hook, waste yarn, and smaller cir, use the crochet provisional method (see Glossary) to CO 136 sts. Place marker (pm) and join for working in the rnd, being careful not to twist sts.

RNDS 1–10: Knit.

RND 11: Purl (turning row).

RNDS 12–21: Knit.

RND 22: Remove provisional CO and place live sts on larger cir. With WS tog, and using larger cir, [knit 1 st from front cir tog with 1 st from back cir] to end of rnd—136 sts.

RND 23: *K17, M1 (see Glossary); rep from * to end—144 sts.

78

SPIDER PATTERN

Work Rnds 1–39 of Spider chart.

SHAPE CROWN

Change to smaller cir needle.
Note: Change to dpns when knitting becomes too tight to work comfortably on cir.

RNDS 1–2: With MC, knit.

RND 3: With B, knit.

RND 4: With B, k10, *k9, sl 2 tog as if to knit, k1, p2sso; rep from * to last two sts, sl 2 tog as if to knit, remove m, k1, p2sso, pm for new beg of rnd—120 sts rem.

RNDS 5–6: With MC, *k9, sl 1. Rep from * to end.

RNDS 7–8: With B, knit.

RNDS 9–10: Rep Rnds 5–6.

RND 11: With B, knit.

RND 12: With B, k8, *sl 2 tog as if to knit, k1, p2sso, k7; rep from * to last 2 sts, sl 2 tog as if to knit, remove m, k1, p2sso, pm for new beg of rnd—96 sts rem.

RNDS 13–14: *With MC, k7, sl 1; rep from * to end.

RNDS 15–16: With B, knit.

RNDS 17–18: Rep Rnds 13–14.

RND 19: With B, knit.

RND 20: With B, k6, *sl 2 tog as if to knit, k1, p2sso, k5, rep from* to last two sts, sl 2 tog as if to knit, remove marker, k1, p2sso, pm for new beg of rnd—72 sts rem.

RNDS 21–22: With MC, *k5, sl 1; rep from * to end.

RNDS 23–24 : With B, knit.

RNDS 25–26: Rep Rnds 17–18.

RND 27: With B, knit.

RND 28: With B, k4, *sl 2 tog as if to knit, k1, p2sso, k3, rep from * to last two sts. Sl 2 as if to knit, remove marker, k1, p2sso, pm—48 sts rem.

RNDS 29–30: With MC, *k3, sl 1, rep from* to end.

RNDS 31–32: With B, knit.

RNDS 33–34: Rep Rnds 25–26.

RND 35: With B, knit.

RND 36: With B, k2, *sl 2 tog as if to knit, k1, p2sso, k1, rep from * to last two sts, sl 2 as if to knit, remove marker, k1, p2sso, pm—24 sts rem.

RNDS 37–38: With MC, *k1, sl 1, rep from * to end.

RND 39: With B, [k2tog] to end—12 sts rem.

RND 40: With B, knit.

RND 41: With B, [k2tog] to end—6 sts rem.

Cut yarn, draw tail through rem stitches, and pull tight to secure. Fasten off inside. Weave in ends.

FINISHING

Lay hat flat and block with steam. (If using a steam iron, do not press iron directly on hat.)

✳ Spinning for Stripes

Spinners have many options for coloring our yarns. For this hat, Nancy created the long repeats of color in the variegated yarn by machine knitting the handspun yarn and dyeing the knitted fabric (see above), a method described in "Machine Knitting to Dye For" (*Spin·Off* Fall 2006, 60–65). She then frogged (ripped) the dyed blank and knitted it again with the black yarn for the color pattern. If you're not prepared to dye your own yarn, you can create a yarn with long repeats of color by working with space-dyed carded roving or combed top. Handpainted roving or top can be spun and knitted as singles or Navajo-plied. You can always knit your handspun yarn using the traditional Fair Isle method: with separate skeins in different solid colors, knitting with only two yarns at a time by stranding them and changing colors at designated intervals.

old garden scarf

{Faina Letoutchaia}

Faina Letoutchaia loves old gardens with overgrown plants and flowers and old terra-cotta pots. These old flowerpots—aged, with cracks and old decoration, moss, even a toad making his home inside—are the inspiration for this shawl. The yarn is spun softly for drape. Designed with angled sections and a gusset on the back, this shawl stays on your shoulders without riding up your neck in the back. This scarf can be a little piece of summer in the dead of the winter, a reminder that summer will bring new flowers into an old garden and old terra-cotta pots.

Spinning Notes

Fiber: 3 oz (85 g) batt of 47% Merino, 33% kid mohair, 20% Tencel.
Drafting method: Short draw.
Spindles: Singles, supported Tibetan spindle; plying, top-whorl spindle.
Singles direction spun: Z.
Singles wraps per inch: 85.
Number of plies: 2.
Plied direction spun: S.
Plied twists per inch: 5.
Plied wraps per inch: 40.
Total yardage: 750 yd (686 m).
Yards per pound: 4,000.

Knitting Notes

Yardage used: 600 yd (549 m).
Yarn classification: Laceweight (Lace #0).
Needles: U.S. size 2 (3 mm). Adjust needle size if necessary to obtain the correct gauge.
Notions: Tapestry needle; crochet cotton; size C/2 (3 mm) crochet hook; stitch markers (m).
Gauge: Exact gauge is not critical for this project. For shawl shown, 32 sts and 44 rows = 4" (10 cm) in St st, before blocking; 30 sts and 48 rows (3 patt reps wide and 4 patt reps high) from Rows 1–12 of Tail chart measure about 4½" (11.5 cm) wide and 6" (15 cm) high, after blocking.
Finished size: 10" (25.5 cm) wide at each end, 13" (33 cm) high in center of middle section, and 76" (193 cm) long measured along outer edge of curve.

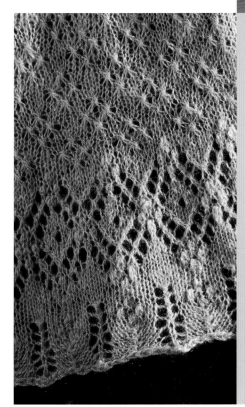

Key

☐	knit on RS; purl on WS
•	purl on RS; knit on WS
O	yo
∕	k2tog
∖	ssk
⋎	p2tog
⋏	k3tog on both RS and WS
⋏	sl 1, k2tog, psso
⋏	sl 2 as if to k2tog, k1, p2sso
v	slipped selvedge st (see instructions)
M	M1P on RS; M1 on WS (see Glossary)
⌑	5-st nupp (see Stitch Guide)
⋏	p5 nupp sts tog on WS
+	work 1 st tog with tail st (see instructions)
⌒	BO 1 st
▨	seed st (see Stitch Guide)
▨	no stitch
☐	pattern repeat
		marker position
⋈₃	spider st (see Stitch Guide)
⋈₉	make 9 sts out of 3 (see Stitch Guide)
⋈₁₁	make 11 sts out of 5 (see Stitch Guide)

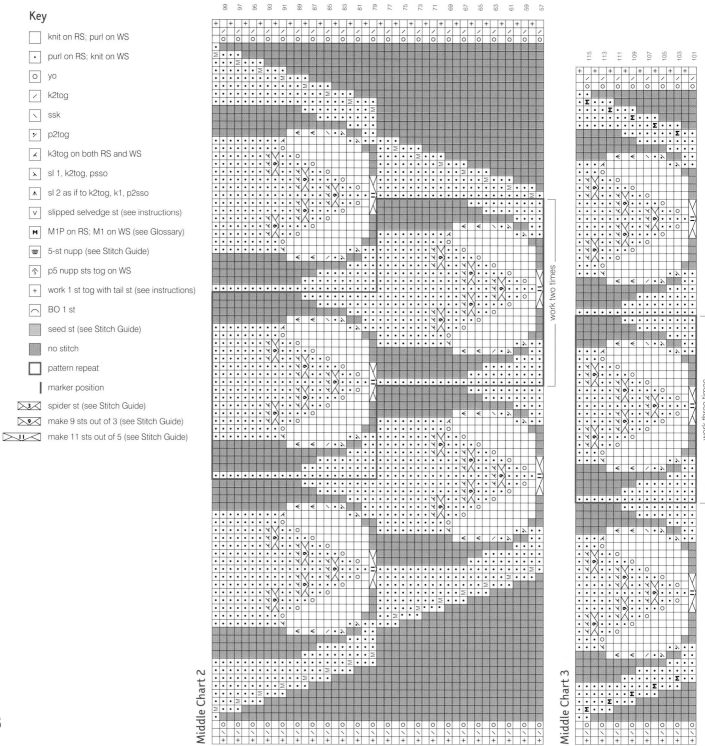

Middle Chart 2

Middle Chart 3

work two times

work three times

MIDDLE SECTION

Carefully undo crochet chain of provisional CO from one tail, leaving waste yarn lifeline in place, and with WS facing, place back loops of 68 revealed sts on needle. Turn work so RS is facing and needle with sts is in left hand. Join yarn to end of sts on needle, and use the knitted method (see Glossary) to CO 15 sts for center section—83 sts on left needle.

Carefully undo crochet chain of provisional CO from other tail, leaving waste yarn lifeline in place, and with WS facing, place back loops of 68 revealed sts on a separate needle that will become the right needle—83 sts on left needle; 68 sts on right needle. Middle section is worked back and forth in rows, joining 1 st of middle section to 1 tail st at the end of each row. Row 1 begins by working the middle section sts on the left needle first.

With RS facing, work Row 1 of Middle Chart 1 (see page 85) over first 14 sts, ssk (last st tog with next tail st), turn—1 st joined from tail. Turn work so WS is facing, work Row 2 of chart over 14 sts, p2tog (last st tog with next tail st), turn—1 st joined from tail. Cont in this manner, working joins as ssk on RS rows and p2tog on WS rows, until Row 56 of chart has been

87

Middle Border

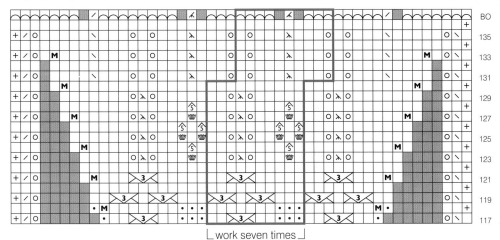

⌐ work seven times ⌐

Key

☐	knit on RS; purl on WS
·	purl on RS; knit on WS
O	yo
╱	k2tog
╲	ssk
⋎	p2tog
⊼	k3tog on both RS and WS
⋏	sl 1, k2tog, psso
⋀	sl 2 as if to k2tog, k1, p2sso
V	slipped selvedge st (see instructions)
M	M1P on RS; M1 on WS (see Glossary)
♛	5-st nupp (see Stitch Guide)
⇑	p5 nupp sts tog on WS
+	work 1 st tog with tail st (see instructions)
⌒	BO 1 st
▨	seed st (see Stitch Guide)
▩	no stitch
☐	pattern repeat
⏐	marker position
⋈3	spider st (see Stitch Guide)
⋈9	make 9 sts out of 3 (see Stitch Guide)
⋈11	make 11 sts out of 5 (see Stitch Guide)

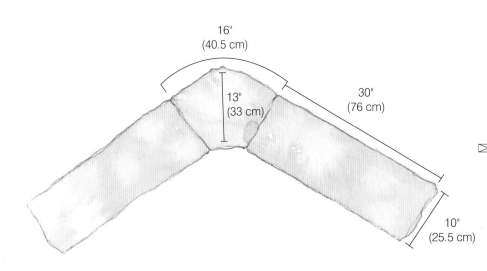

16"
(40.5 cm)

13"
(33 cm)

30"
(76 cm)

10"
(25.5 cm)

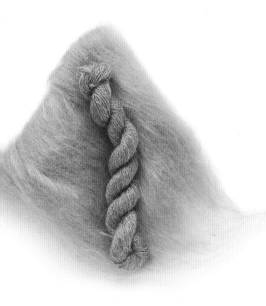

completed—55 sts in middle section; 40 sts rem in each tail.

Work Rows 57–100 of Middle Chart 2—85 sts in middle section; 18 sts rem in each tail. Work Rows 101–116 of Middle Chart 3—95 sts in middle section; 10 sts rem in each tail. Work Rows 117–136 of Middle Border chart—107 sts in middle section; no tail sts rem.

Cut a second strand of yarn about five times the width of the middle section to use for the double strand BO. Using two strands held tog, work BO row of chart, working k2tog or k3tog where indicated while binding off.

FINISHING

Remove waste yarn lifelines. Weave in all ends. Block scarf according to diagram opposite, blocking each tail into a rectangle about 10" (25.5 cm) wide and 30" (76 cm) long and coaxing the middle section into a curve measuring about 16" (40.5 cm) along its BO edge and about 13" (33 cm) high straight up the center.

nordic child's cardigan, hats, and mittens

{Sarah Anderson}

Sarah Anderson created a girl's cardigan in red and natural colors of Bluefaced Leicester with a stranded colorwork motif inspired by her Norwegian heritage. After the cardigan, mittens were a logical pairing, but the set wasn't finished without a matching hat . . . and what a shame not to make a boy's version. When inverted, the heart motif looked to Sarah like little men cheering beside spaceships. A helmet-style hat completed the boy's version. The wide hems cover the stranded colorwork floats to prevent little fingers from snagging.

Spinning Notes

Fiber: Bluefaced Leicester top (ecru, 4.2 oz [119 g]; brown, 8.4 oz [238 g]; oatmeal, 9.1 oz [258 g]; black, 0.4 oz [11 g]; red, 7.1 oz [201 g]).

Shown here: Natural ecru, natural brown, and black top from Ashland Bay; ecru top dyed red after spinning; 25% brown/75% ecru top drumcarded for oatmeal.

Preparation: Top—spun directly from top; batts—separated into strips and spun directly.

Drafting method: Short draw, semiworsted.

Wheel system: Singles—direct drive; plying—bobbin driven.

Ratio (singles/plying): 1:9.

Singles direction spun: Z.

Singles wraps per inch: 30.

Number of plies: 3.

Plied direction spun: S.

Plied twists per inch: 4.

Plied wraps per inch: 14.

Total yardage: Ecru, 277 yd (253 m); brown, 548 yd (501 m); oatmeal, 589 yd (539 m); black, 36 yd (33 m); red, 283 yd (259 m).

Yards per pound: 1,019.

Knitting Notes

Yarn classification: Sportweight (Fine #2).

Yardage used: *Cardigan* (size 3T)—ecru (200 yd [183 m]); natural brown (52 yd [48 m] for girl's version, 465 yd [425 m] for boy's version; oatmeal (465 yd [425 m]) for girl's version, 52 yd [48 m] for boy's version); black (20 yd [18 m]); red (20 yd [18 m]). *Girl's hat*—ecru (77 yd [70 m]); natural brown (20 yd [18 m]); oatmeal (64 yd [59 m]); black (7 yd [6 m]); red (26 yd [24 m]). *Boy's hat*—black (6 yd [5 m]); brown (6 yd [5 m]); oatmeal (3 yd [3 m]); red (173 yd [158 m]). *Mittens* (size 3T)—oatmeal (girl's version only, 5 yd [5 m]); brown (boy's version only, 5 yd [5 m]); black (3 yd [3 m]); red (64 yd [59 m]).

Needles: *Cardigans*—U.S. size 4 (3.5 mm): straight. *Girl's hat*—U.S. size 4 (3.5 mm): straight, and U.S. size 3 (3.25 mm): straight. *Boy's hat*—U.S. size 4 (3.5 mm): 16" (40 cm) circular (cir) and set of 5 double-pointed (dpn). *Mittens*—U.S. size 4 (3.5 mm): set of 4 dpn, and U.S. size 3 (3.25 mm): set of 4 dpn. Adjust needle sizes if necessary to obtain the correct gauge.

Notions: Stitch holders or smooth waste yarn; stitch markers (m); tapestry needle; sewing needle and matching thread; five ¾" (2 cm) buttons for each sweater and 1 button for each hat.

Gauge: 24 sts and 32 rows = 4" (10 cm) on larger needles in texture patt.

Finished size: Cardigan and mitten instructions are written for 12–18 months, 2T, and 3T. Hat instructions are one size (hat circumference about 17" [43 cm]). Pictured here: 2T.

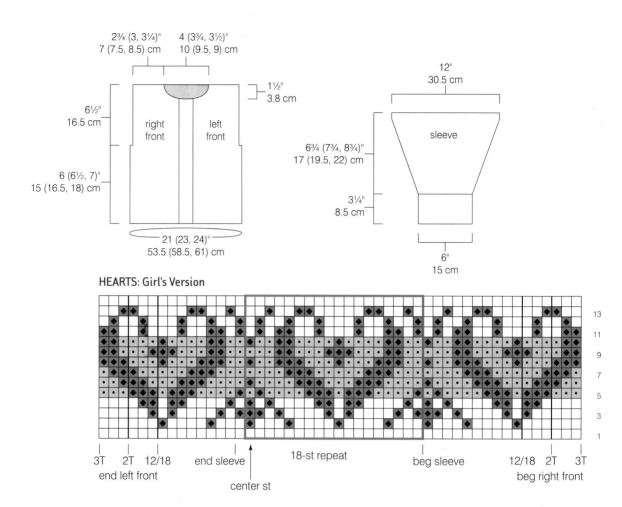

2¾ (3, 3¼)"
7 (7.5, 8.5) cm

4 (3¾, 3½)"
10 (9.5, 9) cm

1½"
3.8 cm

6½"
16.5 cm

right
front

left
front

6 (6½, 7)"
15 (16.5, 18) cm

21 (23, 24)"
53.5 (58.5, 61) cm

12"
30.5 cm

sleeve

6¾ (7¾, 8¾)"
17 (19.5, 22) cm

3¼"
8.5 cm

6"
15 cm

HEARTS: Girl's Version

13
11
9
7
5
3
1

3T   2T   12/18   end sleeve   18-st repeat   beg sleeve   12/18   2T   3T
end left front   ↑   beg right front
                                            center st

HEARTS: Boy's Version

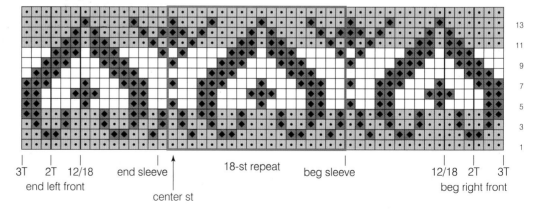

13
11
9
7
5
3
1

3T   2T   12/18   end sleeve   18-st repeat   beg sleeve   12/18   2T   3T
end left front   ↑   beg right front
                                            center st

92

Key

- ☐ ecru
- ◆ natural brown
- ⊡ oatmeal
- ☐ pattern repeat

TEXTURE: Girl's Version

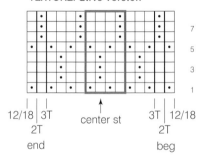

12/18 | 3T | center st | 3T | 12/18
2T | | | 2T
end | | beg

TEXTURE: Boy's Version

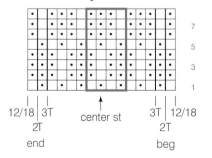

12/18 | 3T | center st | 3T | 12/18
2T | | | 2T
end | | beg

- ☐ knit on RS; purl on WS
- ⊡ purl on RS; knit on WS

CARDIGAN

Hem

With ecru and straight needles, CO 123 (129, 135) sts. Work 20 rows in St st.

ROW 21: (RS) K15, [M1, k31 (33, 35)] three times, M1, k to end—127 (133, 139) sts.

ROW 22: With red, purl.

girl's sweater only

ROW 23: (turning row) K1, *yo, k2tog; rep from * to end.

boy's sweater only

ROW 23: (turning row) Purl.

both sizes

ROW 24: (WS) Purl.

Body

ROW 25: With oatmeal (girl's version) or brown (boy's version), knit.

ROWS 26–27: Work Rows 1–2 of Texture chart for girl's or boy's version.

ROW 28: With brown (girl's version) or oatmeal (boy's version), purl.

ROWS 29–30: With black, knit.

ROWS 31–44: Work Rows 1–14 of Hearts chart.

ROWS 45–46: With black, knit.

ROW 47: With brown (girl's version) or oatmeal (boy's version), knit.

With oatmeal (girl's version) or brown (boy's version), work Texture chart for girl's or boy's version from Row 1 until piece measures 6 (6½, 7)" (15 [16.5, 18] cm) from red turning row.

93

Armholes

With RS facing and continuing to work Texture chart, work 27 (29, 31) sts and place them on a holder for right front, BO 4 sts, work 65 (67, 69) sts in patt and place on a holder for back, BO 4 sts, work rem 27 (29, 31) sts for left front.

Left front

Continue working Texture chart until armhole measures 5" (12.5 cm), ending on neck edge after a RS row. Left front measures 11 (11½, 12)" (28 [29, 30.5] cm) from turning row.

shape neck

ROW 1: BO 3 sts, work in patt to end—24 (26, 28) sts rem.

ROW 2 AND ALL RS ROWS: Work even as established.

ROWS 3, 5, AND 7: BO 2 sts at beg of row, work in patt to end—18 (20, 22) sts rem after Row 7.

ROWS 9 AND 11: BO 1 st, work in patt to end—16 (18, 20) sts rem.

ROW 12: Work even as established.

Place rem 16 (18, 20) sts on holder for shoulder seam.

Right Front

Rejoin yarn at armhole edge. Continue working Texture chart until armhole measures 5" (12.5 cm), ending on neck edge after a WS row.

shape neck

ROW 1: BO 3 sts, work in patt to end—24 (26, 28) sts rem.

ROW 2 AND ALL WS ROWS: Work even in patt as established.

ROWS 3, 5, AND 7: BO 2 sts at beg of row, work in patt to end—18 (20, 22) sts rem after Row 7.

ROWS 9 AND 11: BO 1 st, work in patt to end—16 (18, 20) sts rem.

ROW 12: Work even in patt as established. Place rem 16 (18, 20) sts on holder for shoulder seam.

Back

Rejoin yarn at armhole and work in texture pattern until armhole measures 6½" (16.5 cm), ending shoulders after same patt row as fronts. Back measures 12½ (13, 13½)" (31.5 [33, 34.5] cm) from red hem.

Join Shoulders

Replace held front sts on needle so that RS is ready to be worked. With RS facing out, hold left front shoulder sts tog with back sts. Beginning at shoulder edge, use the three-needle method (see Glossary) to join 16 (18, 20) sts of front and back. BO 33 (31, 29) back neck sts. Replace 16 (18, 20) held right front sts on needles so that RS is ready to be worked and use three-needle method to BO rem sts of front and back.

Sleeves

With ecru, loosely CO 34 sts. Work 20 rows in St st.
ROW 21: (RS) K5 [M1, k8] twice, M1 (see Glossary), k5—37 sts.
ROW 22: With red, purl.

girl's version only
ROW 23: K1, *yo, k2tog; rep from * to end.

boy's version only
ROW 23: Purl.

both versions
ROW 24: Purl.
ROW 25: With oatmeal (girl's version) or brown (boy's version), knit.
ROWS 26–27: Work Rows 1–2 of Texture chart for girl's or boy's version.
ROW 28: With brown (girl's version) or

oatmeal (boy's version), purl.
ROWS 29–30: With black, knit.
ROWS 31–44: Work Rows 1–14 of sleeve portion of boy's or girl's Hearts chart.
ROWS 45–46: With black, knit.
ROW 47: With brown (girl's version) or oatmeal (boy's version), knit.

size 12–18 months only
NEXT ROW: (inc row) K1, M1 (see Glossary), work in Texture patt to last st, M1, k1—2 sts inc'd.

Work 3 rows even.

Rep inc row on next row, then every 4th row five more times, then every 3rd row nine times, working inc'd sts into patt—69 sts.

size 2T only
NEXT ROW: (inc row) K1, M1, work in Texture patt to last st, M1, k1—2 sts inc'd. Work 3 rows even.

Rep inc row on next row, then every 4th row fourteen more times, working inc'd sts into patt—69 sts.

size 3T only

NEXT ROW: (inc row) K1, M1, work in Texture patt to last st, M1, k1—2 sts inc'd. Work 4 rows even.

Rep inc row on next row, then every 5th row four more times, then every 4th row 10 times, working inc'd sts into patt—69 sts. After finishing increases, work in patt until sleeve measures 10 (11, 12)" (25.5 [28, 30.5] cm) from turning row. BO loosely.

Finishing
buttonband

With ecru (girl's version) or red (boy's version), CO 10 sts and work in [k1, p1] rib to fit from neck edge to turning row. Place these 10 sts on a holder and use mattress st (see Glossary) to sew buttonband to left front (girl's version) or right front (boy's version). With pins, mark placement for 5 buttons; place bottom button 1 (¾, 1)" (2.5 [2, 2.5] cm) above turning row, then space rem buttons 2¼ (2½, 2½)" (5.5 [6.5, 6.5 cm) apart.

buttonhole band

Work as for buttonband to 1 (¾, 1)" (2.5, [2, 2.5] cm). Work buttonholes as foll:

ROW 1: Work 4 sts in rib, BO 2 sts, work 4 sts in rib.

ROW 2: Work 4 sts in rib, CO 2 sts over BO sts, work 4 sts in rib.

Use mattress st to sew buttonhole band to front opposite buttonband.

collar

With RS of sweater facing, replace 10 held front band sts on needles and work them in rib patt, pick up and knit (see Glossary) 14 (15, 16) sts along right front neck edge, pick up and knit 34 (32, 30) sts along back neck, pick up and knit 14 (15, 16) sts along left front neck edge, replace 10 held front band sts on needles and work them in rib patt—82 sts. *Note:* Because collar will be turned down, RS of sweater is WS of collar.

NEXT ROW: (RS) [K1, p1] four times, k2tog, [p1, k1] thirty-one times, p2tog, [k1, p1] four times—80 sts rem.

Note: These decreases should eliminate the bump where front bands were attached to sweater fronts.

Work [k1, p1] rib for 1¾" (4.5 cm), ending after a WS row.

collar edge

ROW 1: (RS) With brown (girl's version) or oatmeal (boy's version), knit.

ROW 2: With oatmeal (girl's version) or brown (boy's version), work [k1, p1] to end.

ROW 3: [P1, k1] to end.

ROW 4: With red (girl's version) or black (boy's version), purl.

BO all sts loosely purlwise.

With mattress st, sew sleeve underarms. Sew sleeves into armholes. Loosely whipstitch (see Glossary) sleeve and body hems to allow for stretch. Weave in ends. Sew on buttons. Wash to block, shape, and lay flat to dry.

Key

- ☐ ecru
- ◆ natural brown
- ▣ oatmeal
- ☐ pattern repeat

HEARTS: Girl's Hat

13
11
9
7
5
3
1

end

18-st repeat

beg

GIRL'S HAT

Hem

With larger needles and ecru, CO 71 sts.
Work 20 rows in St st.

ROW 21: (RS) K20, M1, k31, M1, k20—
73 sts.

picot edge

ROW 22: (WS) With red, purl.

ROW 23: K1, *yo, k2tog; rep from * to end.

ROW 24: Purl.

Body

ROW 25: With oatmeal, knit.

ROWS 26-27: Work Rows 1–2 of Texture chart (girl's version).

ROW 28: (WS) With brown, purl.

ROWS 29-30: With black, knit.

ROWS 31-44: Work Rows 1–14 of Hat chart.

ROWS 45-46: With black, knit.

ROW 47: (RS) With brown, k4 [M1, k5] thirteen times, M1, k4—87 sts.

With oatmeal, work in girl's Texture patt until hat measures 6½" (16.5 cm) from turning row, ending after a WS row.

97

Welt

ROWS 1 AND 2: With red, knit.
ROW 3: Purl.
ROW 4: Knit.
With WS facing and smaller needle, pick up 87 sts in purl bumps of Row 1 of welt (first red row). Hold smaller needle behind larger needle and [knit 1 st from front needle tog with 1 st from back needle] to end.

Back of Hat

ROW 1 AND ALL ODD-NUMBERED ROWS: (WS) Purl.
ROW 2: K16, [k2tog, k11] two times, sl 1, k2tog, psso, [k11, ssk] two times, k16—81 sts rem.
ROW 4: K15, [k2tog, k10] two times, sl 1, k2tog, psso, [k10, ssk] two times, k15—75 sts rem.
ROW 6: K14, [k2tog, k9] two times, sl 1, k2tog, psso, [k9, ssk] two times, k14—69 sts rem.

ROW 8: K13, [k2tog, k8] two times, sl 1, k2tog, psso, [k8, ssk] two times, k13—63 sts rem.
ROW 10: K12, [k2tog, k7] two times, sl 1, k2tog, psso, [k7, ssk] two times, k12—57 sts rem.
Continue as established, working one fewer st before first dec and after last dec and one fewer st between decs on each dec row, three more times—39 sts rem.
ROW 18: K2, k2tog, k4, [k3tog, k2] two times, sl 1, k2tog, psso, (k2, k3tog tbl) two times, k4, ssk, k2—27 sts rem.
ROW 20: K2, k2tog, k2, [k2tog, k1] two times, sl 1, k2tog, psso, [k1, ssk] two times, k2, ssk, k2—19 sts rem.
ROW 22: K4, [k2tog] two times, sl 1, k2tog, psso, [ssk] two times, k4—13 sts rem.
ROW 24: [K2tog] two times, k1, sl 1, k2tog, psso, k1, [ssk] two times—7 sts rem.
ROW 26: K2tog, sl 1, k2tog, psso, ssk—3 sts rem.

ROW 27: P3tog. Fasten off rem st. Weave in ends. Whipstitch hem to body, leaving sides open to pick up sts on these edges.

Hat Edge

ROW 1: With RS facing and ecru, pick up and knit 30 stitches along bottom right edge, pick up and knit 31 sts from back edge, pick up and knit 30 sts along bottom left edge—91 sts.
ROW 2: (WS) K2tog, k28, place marker (pm), [p1, k2tog] ten times, p1, pm, k28, k2tog—79 sts rem.
ROW 3: (dec row) K2, k2tog, k25, [k1, p1] ten times, k1, k25, k2tog, k2—77 sts rem.
ROW 4: K28, [p1, k1] ten times, p1, k28.
ROW 5: (dec row) K2tog, k26, [k1, p1] ten times, k1, k26, k2tog—75 sts rem.
ROW 6: K27, [p1, k1] ten times, p1, k27.
Continue as established, working one fewer st before first m and one fewer st after second m on every dec rnd, for 5 more rows—69 sts rem after Row 11.
ROW 12: BO in patt to last 10 sts, work [k1, p1] rib to end—10 sts rem.
Work [k1, p1] rib over rem sts for 4½" (11.5 cm) or to desired chin strap length to buttonhole. (Try the hat on the child for size if possible.)

buttonhole

ROW 1: Work 4 sts in patt, BO 2 sts, work 4 sts in patt.
ROW 2: Work 4 sts in patt, CO 2 sts over BO sts, work 4 sts in patt.
Continue in rib for ¾" (2 cm). BO sts in patt.

Finishing

Sew up the sides of the hem. Sew button to cap opposite buttonhole for chin strap. Weave in loose ends. Wash and block hat.

BOY'S HAT

With red and dpn, CO 4 sts. Work I-cord (see Glossary) for 2 rows.

NEXT ROW: [K1f&b] four times—8 sts. Divide sts evenly over 4 dpns and join for working in the rnd.

RND 1: Knit.

RND 2: [K1, M1, k1] four times—12 sts. Place marker (pm) before last st.

RND 3: [K1, M1, k1, M1, k1] four times—20 sts.

RND 4: (K1, M1, knit to end of dpn) four times—24 sts.

Rep Rnd 4 until there are 30 sts on each needle—120 sts total.

Purl 3 rnds.

With cir, work [k1, p1] rib for 2¾" (7 cm). End last rnd 5 sts before end of rnd. Place the next 40 sts (5 sts from end of rnd, 35 sts from next rnd) on hold for front of hat. Turn work.

NEXT ROW: (WS) Ssk, work in rib to end—1 st dec'd.

Rep last row nine more times, keeping sts in patt—70 sts rem.

NEXT ROW: (WS) Ssk, work in patt over next 48 sts, place last 30 worked sts on hold for back of hat, work rem 20 sts in patt to end of row.

Left Earflap

NEXT ROW: (RS) Ssk, work 18 sts in [k1, p1] rib, turn—1 st dec'd.

Rep last row until 10 sts rem. Break yarn, leaving a 12" (30.5 cm) tail. Place rem 10 sts on hold.

Right Earflap

Rejoin yarn at the back neck side of the ear flap. Work as for left flap, but leave rem sts on needle; do not break yarn.

With RS facing, pick up and knit 15 sts

along front edge of right earflap, knit 40 held sts for front of hat, pick up and knit 15 sts along front edge of left earflap, knit 10 held sts from left earflap, pick up and knit 7 sts along back of left earflap, knit 30 held sts for back of hat, pick up and knit 7 sts from back of right earflap, k10 right earflap sts—134 sts.

Edge

RND 1: With oatmeal, k10, k2tog, k1, k2tog, k9, [k2tog, k8] two times, k2tog, k9, k2tog, k1, k2tog, k25, k2tog, k1, [k2tog, k11] two times, k2tog, k1, k2tog, k15—122 sts rem.

RND 2: With brown, [k1, p1] to end.

RND 3: [P1, k1] to end.

RND 4: With black, knit.

BO all sts purlwise.

Strap

With RS facing and red, pick up and knit 10 sts along bottom edge of right earflap. Work in [k1, p1] rib for 4" (10 cm) or to desired chin strap length to buttonhole. (Try the hat on the child for size if possible.)

Buttonhole

ROW 1: Work 4 sts in patt, BO 2 sts, work 4 sts in patt.

ROW 2: Work 4 sts in patt, CO 2 sts over BO sts, work 4 sts in patt.

Continue in patt for ½" (1.3 cm). BO sts in patt.

Finishing

Sew button to left earflap. Weave in ends. *Note:* Blocking is important on this hat; wash it and allow to dry with a ball or balloon inside it to round out the top.

shape top

RND 1: Needle 1—k1, sl 1, k1, psso, knit to last 3 sts, k2tog, k1; Needle 2—k1, sl 1, k1, psso, knit to end; Needle 3—knit to last 3 sts, k2tog, k1—4 sts dec'd.

RND 2: Knit.

Rep Rnds 1 and 2 four (four, five) more times—10 (11, 8) sts rem.

NEXT ROUND: [K2tog] five (five, four) times, k0 (1, 0)—5 (6, 4) sts rem.

Cut yarn and draw tail through rem sts. Pull tight to gather and fasten off on WS.

thumb

Arrange 9 held thumb sts on two larger dpns; with third dpn and red, pick up and knit 5 sts over CO sts—14 sts.

NEXT RND: Knit to last 6 sts, k2tog, k2, k2tog—12 sts rem.

Knit until thumb measures 1" (2.5 cm) from picked-up sts. *Note:* You may want to work a few extra rnds for larger sizes.

NEXT RND: [K2tog] six times—6 sts rem.

Cut yarn and draw tail through rem sts. Pull tight to gather and fasten off on WS.

Left Mitten

Work as for right mitten to thumb gusset.

thumb gusset

RND 1: Knit to last 2 sts, [M1, k1] two times—32 (33, 34) sts.

RNDS 2, 4, AND 6: Knit.

RND 3: Knit to last 4 sts, M1, k3, M1, k1—34 (35, 36) sts.

RND 5: Knit to last 6 sts, M1, k5, M1, k1—36 (37, 38) sts.

RND 7: Knit to last 9 sts, place 9 sts on hold for thumb, CO 3 sts, knit to end—30 (31, 32) sts.

Continue as for right mitten.

Finishing

Weave in ends. Block as desired.

MITTENS

Left Mitten

With red and larger dpns, CO 32 (33, 34) sts. Divide over 3 dpns and join for working in the rnd, being careful not to twist sts.

RND 1: Purl.

RND 2: With oatmeal (girl's version) or brown (boy's version), knit.

RNDS 3 AND 5: [K1, p1] sixteen (sixteen, seventeen) times, k0 (1, 0).

RND 4: [P1, k1] sixteen (sixteen, seventeen) times, p0 (1, 0).

RND 6: With black, knit.

RND 7: Purl.

RND 8: With red, k6 (7, 7), k2tog, k15, k2tog, knit to end—30 (31, 32) sts.

RNDS 9–14: With smaller needles, [k1, p1] fifteen (fifteen, sixteen) times, k0 (1, 0).

RND 15: With larger needles, knit. Rearrange sts as foll: Needle 1—15 (15, 16) sts; Needle 2—8 sts; Needle 3—7 (8, 8) sts.

thumb gusset

RND 1: [K1, M1] two times, knit to end—32 (33, 34) sts.

RNDS 2, 4, AND 6: Knit.

RND 3: K1, M1, k3, M1, knit to end—34 (35, 36) sts.

RND 5: K1, M1, k5, M1, knit to end—36 (37, 38) sts.

RND 7: Place 9 sts on holder for thumb, CO 3 sts, knit to end—30 (31, 32) sts.

Knit even until mitten measures 4 (4¼, 4½)" (10 [11, 11.5] cm) or 1" (2.5 cm) less than desired length.

100

✳ Kool-Aid Dyeing

This children's set began as an experiment in Kool-aid dyeing, aiming for "an explosion of many colors—Kool-aid colors." Dyeing with Kool-aid is very simple. To get the saturation of color of the red yarn, Sarah used 3 packets of unsweetened Tropical Punch or Cherry Kool-aid per ounce of yarn. (Although Kool-aid is a food-safe dye, it is not recommended to use any dyeing equipment for any other purpose.)

To begin, soak the skein to be dyed in warm water with 4–5 tablespoons of vinegar for about a half hour. Squeeze out the water and lay the skein in a shallow glass pan like a lasagna pan.

Mix Kool-aid with warm water and 4–5 tablespoons of vinegar; make enough mixture to cover the skein. Pour this mixture over the yarn, being sure that all fiber is well-covered. Cover the dish with plastic wrap to form a seal. Use the microwave oven to get the dyebath very hot without boiling, then keep it hot for about 30 minutes to set the dye: Microwave on high for 3 minutes. After 3 minutes, Sarah recommends setting the microwave at power level 4 for 20 minutes; if your microwave doesn't have power settings, it may be necessary to run it for 1–2 minutes at a time, allowing it to sit for 1 minute between heating times. Allow the whole pan to cool to room temperature or overnight.

Remove the cooled yarn from the dyebath and wash with soap and a warm rinse to be sure any stray dye is removed. Press out excess water in a towel and air-dry.

101

sheepy mittens

{Amy King}

Inspired by a sampler of natural-colored Shetland available in her shop, Amy King created this pattern to show off some of her favorite wool. After sampling both two-ply and three-ply versions of the yarn, she selected the three-ply, which made the sheep "pop" and created well-defined lines. The pattern celebrates the varied colors of Shetland fleece (and can be forgiving of the lumps and bumps that are common in a beginner's yarn).

Spinning Notes

Fiber: Shetland combed top—2 oz (57 g) in each of 4 colors (black, brown, white, and gray).

Preparation: Predrafted.

Drafting method: Short draw.

Wheel system: Singles—double drive; plying—scotch tension.

Ratio (singles/plying): 19:1.

Singles direction spun: Z.

Number of plies: 3.

Plied direction spun: S.

Plied twists per inch: 5.

Plied wraps per inch: 13.

Total yardage: 130 yd (119 m) of each color.

Yards per pound: 1,040.

Knitting Notes

Yarn classification: Sportweight (Fine #2).

Yardage used: 206 yd [188 m] total; about 68 yd (62 m) black, 36 yd (33 m) gray, 38 yd (35 m) brown, and 64 yd (59 m) white.

Needles: U.S. 3 (3.25 mm): set of 4 or 5 double-pointed (dpn). Adjust needle size if necessary to obtain the correct gauge.

Notions: Waste yarn; tapestry needle; stitch markers (m).

Gauge: 12 sts and 12 rnds = 2" (5 cm).

Finished size: 7½" (19 cm) hand circumference and 10" (25.5 cm) from cuff to top.

Cuff

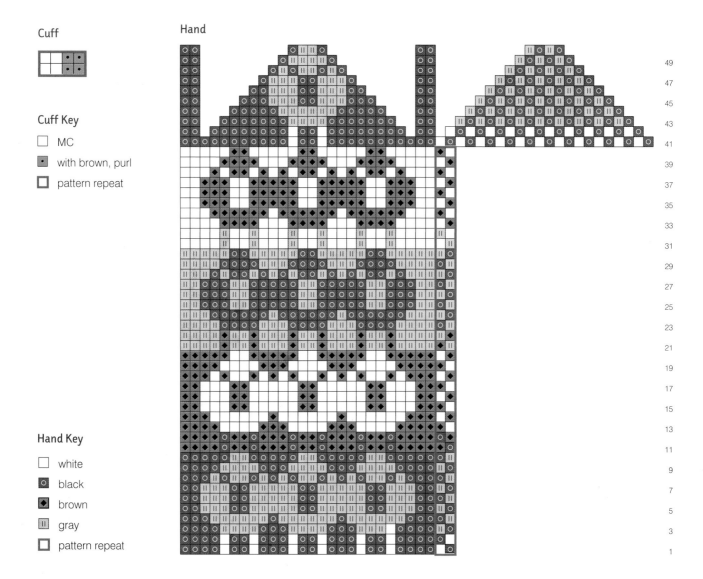

Cuff Key

☐ MC

▨ with brown, purl

☐ pattern repeat

Hand

Hand Key

☐ white

◉ black

◆ brown

‖ gray

☐ pattern repeat

49
47
45
43
41
39
37
35
33
31
29
27
25
23
21
19
17
15
13
11
9
7
5
3
1

RIGHT MITTEN

Cuff

With black and a stretchy method such as cable or long-tail (see Glossary), CO 48 sts. Join for working in the rnd, being careful not to twist sts. Work Cuff chart.

RND 1: *With white, k2, with black, p2; rep from * to end.

Rep Rnd 1 for fourteen more rnds; piece measures about 2¼" (5.5 cm).

NEXT RND: With black, knit.

Hand

Note: Place marker (pm) after 22 sts.

RND 1: Work 2-st rep of Hand chart to m, work Hand chart to end of rnd.

Work Rnds 2–19 of Hand chart.

RND 20: (thumb rnd) With waste yarn, k8, sl 8 sts back to left needle, work Hand chart to end of rnd.

Work Rnds 21–41 of Hand chart.

RND 42: Maintaining color patt as given on chart, ssk, work chart to 2 sts before m, k2tog, k2, ssk, knit to last 4 sts, k2tog, k2—4 sts dec'd.

RNDS 43–50: Maintaining color patt, rep Rnd 42 eight more times—12 sts rem after Rnd 50.

With black, knit 1 rnd.

Cut yarn, leaving a 12" (30.5 cm) tail. Arrange sts so that 6 sts from back of mitten are on one dpn and rem 6 sts from palm are on another. With tail threaded on a tapestry needle, use Kitchener st (see Glossary) to graft sts tog.

Thumb

Remove the waste yarn from thumb and arrange 16 revealed sts over 3 dpns.

RND 1: Beg with lower set of sts and [with white, k1; with brown, k1] four times, with white, M1 (see Glossary) at edge of thumb, [with brown, k1; with white, k1] four times, with brown, M1—18 sts.

RND 2: [With brown, k1; with white, k1] nine times.

RND 3: [With white, k1; with brown, k1] nine times.

Rep Rnds 2–3 until thumb measures 2" (5 cm).

shape tip

RND 1: Maintaining color pattern, [k1, k2tog] six times—12 sts rem.

RND 2: Work even in patt as established.

RND 3: [K2tog] six times—6 sts rem.

Cut both yarns, leaving an 8" (20.5 cm) tail. Draw one tail through rem sts, pull tight, and fasten off inside.

LEFT MITTEN

Work as for Right Mitten through Rnd 19 of Hand chart.

RND 20: (thumb rnd) Work 14 sts of Hand chart, with waste yarn, k8, sl 8 sts back to left needle, work Hand chart to end. Work rest of mitten as for Right Mitten.

FINISHING

Weave in ends. Block mittens as desired.

chutes and ladders hat

{Kristi R. Schueler}

Cables and dropped stitches come together for a fun and quick project suitable for spinners of any skill. The extra loft of the bulky two-ply fills the spaces of the dropped stitches and traps more air in the yarn, resulting in a warmer hat with less weight. The drumcarded fiber spun with a supported long backward draw made soft, airy singles. Kristi Schueler preserved the color layers in the batts by tearing the batt into a continuous roving.

Spinning Notes

Fiber: 6 oz (170 g) blended wool batts.

Shown here: 4 TerraBellaSpun Batts (10% Black Welsh Mountain/70% Merino/20% superwash wool), Rainforest colorway.

Preparation: Batts torn into continuous roving and predrafted.

Drafting method: Supported long backward draw.

Wheel system: Scotch tension.

Ratio (singles/plying): 4:1/7:1.

Singles direction spun: Z.

Singles twists per inch: 2.

Singles wraps per inch: 9.

Twist angle: 30°.

Number of plies: 2.

Plied direction spun: S.

Plied twists per inch: .75–1.25.

Plied wraps per inch: 3–4.

Total yardage: 150 yd (137 m).

Yards per pound: 400 yd.

Knitting Notes

Yarn classification: Very bulky (Super Bulky #6).

Yardage used: 35 (45, 60) yd (32 [41, 55] m).

Needles: U.S. size 11 (8.0 mm): set of 4 double-pointed (dpn). Adjust needle size if necessary to obtain the correct gauge.

Notions: Cable needle (cn); stitch marker (m); tapestry needle.

Gauge: 12 sts and 13 rnds = 4" (10 cm) in Chutes and Ladders pattern.

Finished size: 14 (16, 18)" (35.5 [40.5, 45.5] cm) head circumference; 6 (7¼, 8½)" (15 [18.5, 21.5] cm) tall.

107

stitch guide Chutes and Ladders

(multiple of 6 sts)

SET-UP RND: *[Yo] twice, BO 2 sts, k4; rep from * to end of rnd.

RNDS 1–2: *K4, drop the double yo from needle, [yo] twice, k1; rep from * to end of rnd.

RND 3: *Sl 2 sts to cn and hold to front, k2, k2 from cn, drop double yo from needle, [yo] twice; rep from * to end of rnd.

RND 4: *K4, drop the double yo from needle, [yo] twice, k1; rep from * to end of rnd.

Rep Rnds 1—4 for patt.

Tearing Batts into Roving

Before spinning, Kristi turned each batt into a continuous piece of roving. She started by tearing a lengthwise strip 2 to 3 inches wide from top to bottom in the same direction as the grain of the batt. She stopped when the tear was about the same distance from the bottom of the batt as the strip was thick. She then moved over 2 to 3 inches and started a new tear in the batt, this time working from bottom to top, once again stopping before the top of the batt. She continued making these zigzag tears until one long strip of fiber was formed.

108

BRIM

Using long-tail method, CO 42 (48, 54) sts. Distribute sts evenly on 3 or 4 needles, place marker (pm), and join for working in the rnd, being careful not to twist sts.

Work [k2, p1] rib for 4 rnds.

BODY

Beginning with Set-up rnd, work Chutes and Ladders pattern. Work Rnds 1–4 three (four, five) times. Work Rnds 1–3 once more; hat measures about 5 (6¼, 7½)" (12.5 [16, 19] cm) from CO edge.

CROWN

NEXT RND: *Drop double yo, yo, k2tog, k2; rep from * to end of rnd—28 (32, 36) sts rem.

NEXT RND: *Drop single yo, yo, k1, ssk; rep from * to end of rnd—21 (24, 27) sts rem.

NEXT RND: *Drop single yo, k2tog; rep from * to end of rnd—7 (8, 9) sts rem.

LAST RND: [K2tog] to end of rnd, ending k1 (0, 1)—4 (4, 5) sts rem.

FINISHING

Cut yarn, thread tail on tapestry needle and draw through rem sts, pulling tight to close hole. Weave in ends and block as desired.

square bags that look round

{Sarah Swett}

You may be reminded of the book *Charlie and the Chocolate Factory* when knitting one of these little bags, which start with a simple bias square. As stitches are picked up from the four sides, a round-bottomed bag emerges, perfect for carrying a supported spindle or two, a little wooden bowl, and a bit of roving yet to be spun. Sarah Swett enjoys the "pure, rhythmic pleasure" and whirling sound made by a supported spindle turning in the bottom of a wooden bowl in her lap.

Spinning Notes

Fiber: 1 oz (28 g) each of white, brown, and green cotton sliver.

Shown here: Fox Fibre Cotton Sliver.

Drafting method: One-handed long draw.

Spindle: Supported spindle with bowl.

Singles direction spun: Z.

Singles wraps per inch: 75.

Number of plies: 4.

Plied direction spun: S.

Plied twists per inch: 5.

Plied wraps per inch: 21–24.

Total yardage: 394 yd (360 m).

Yards per pound: 2,100.

Knitting Notes

Yarn classification: Fingering weight (Super Fine #1).

Yardage used: 50 yd (46 m) each of white and brown for striped and argyle bags; 26 yd (24 m) green for striped bag only.

Needles: U.S. size 2 (2.75 mm): set of 5 double-pointed (dpn). Adjust needle size if necessary to obtain the correct gauge.

Gauge: Striped bag—12 sts and 18 rnds = 2" (5 cm). Argyle bag—14 sts and 17 rnds = 2" (5 cm).

Notions: Small safety pin; tapestry needle.

Finished size: Striped bag—5¾" (14.5 cm) wide and 6½" (16.5 cm) tall. Argyle bag— 5½" (14 cm) wide and 7" (18 cm) tall.

111

Argyle 1

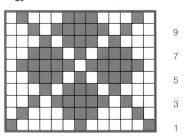

9
7
5
3
1

Key

☐ white
▓ brown
☐ pattern repeat

BAG

Bottom

With brown (argyle) bag or green (striped bag), CO 3 sts. Do not join.

ROW 1: K1, M1 (see Glossary), k2—4 sts.
ROW 2: K1, M1, k3—5 sts.
ROWS 3–28: K1, M1, knit to end—31 sts at the end of Row 28.
ROWS 29–32: Knit.
  With brown yarn (both bags), dec as foll:
ROWS 33–60: K1, ssk, knit to end—3 sts rem at the end of Row 60. Leave on needle.

Sides

With brown (argyle bag) or green (striped bag), pick up and knit (see Glossary) 69 sts evenly around edges of square, arrange evenly on 4 dpns—72 sts. Join for working in the rnd.

argyle bag only

SET-UP RND: Purl.
RNDS 1–31: Work Argyle chart three times, then rep Rnd 1 once more.

striped bag only

RND 1: With green, purl.
RNDS 2–16: With brown, knit.
RND 17: Purl.
RNDS 18–22: With white, knit.
RND 23: Purl.
RNDS 24–25: With green, knit.
RND 26: Purl.
RND 27: With white, knit.
RND 28: Purl.
RNDS 29–35: With brown, knit.
RND 36: With green, knit.
RND 37: Purl.

Top

RNDS 1–2: With white, knit.
RND 3: *K4, yo, ssk; rep from * to end.
RND 4: Knit.
RND 5: Purl.
Rep Rnds 4–5 three more times.
  Using applied I-cord method (see Glossary) to work a 3-st I-cord, BO sts. Weave in ends.

FINISHING

Make two 17" (43 cm) 3-st I-cords (see Glossary) for each bag (1 green and 1 brown for striped bag; 1 white and 1 brown for argyle bag). Do not BO; place sts on a safety pin. Thread through holes and graft BO and CO ends of each I-cord tog using Kitchener st (see Glossary) to make 2 loops, one of each color. Pull on both loops to close the bag.
  Wash in warm soapy water. Dry flat.

112

✳ Plying From a Ball

Sarah plied four strands of singles together following the advice of Ed Franquemont, who suggested plying the Andean way, using two steps when plying on a spindle. Wind the singles into a center-pull ball. Though Ed used his wrist to make a two-ended ball, a ballwinder or nøstepinne works well, too. (Slide the ball onto a piece of rolled cardboard or a paper tube to keep the inside from collapsing and tangling.) Pull the strands from the inside and outside of the ball and hold them together to wind another center-pull ball. (A gentle squeeze on the cardboard will release the inside strands.) For a two-ply yarn, stop here and add plying twist. For four plies, wind a third center-pull ball with all four strands held parallel. Ply these four strands by adding twist with a wheel or spindle. No tangles or eyelashes!

113

indigo and lichen beret

{by Jeannine Bakriges}

The Indigo and Lichen Beret is based on a handspun beret that Jeannine Bakriges received as a gift. The piece begins from the middle of the knitted circle and grows outward, eventually incorporating a color pattern that frames the face. It is finished with an I-cord edging that provides a snug but comfortable fit. The color pattern, which evokes a flowering thistle, combines yarns that were nature-dyed with indigo and lichens. The spindle-spun singles were then wound into two balls and threaded through the drainage holes of two clay flowerpots to be plied.

Spinning Notes

Fiber: 3 oz (85 g) carded British longwool roving like Bluefaced Leicester, Wensleydale, or Cotswold; 1 oz (28.5 g) silk/wool top.

Preparation: Wool roving—split in half and predrafted. Silk/wool top—split into smaller sections and predrafted.

Drafting method: Short forward/ backward combination draw.

Spindles: Low whorl.

Singles direction spun: Z.

Number of plies: 2.

Plied direction spun: S.

Plied twists per inch: 4.

Plied wraps per inch: 20.

Total yardage: 160 yd (146 m) wool; 5 yd (4.6 m) silk/wool in each of 6 colors (or one 30 yd [27 m] space-dyed skein).

Yards per pound: 850 (wool).

Knitting Notes

Yarn classification: Sportweight (Light #2).

Yardage used: 152 yd (139 m) wool; 5 yd (4.6 m) silk/wool in each of 6 colors.

Needles: U.S. size 3 (3.25 mm): set of 5 double-pointed (dpn) and 16" (40 cm) circular (cir) of same size. Adjust needle size if necessary to obtain the correct gauge.

Gauge: 12 sts and 16 rnds = 2" (5 cm). *Note:* Exact gauge is not critical for this project, as beret size can be adjusted by working more or fewer rnds.

Finished size: 5¼" (13.5 cm) from middle of crown to fold of blocked beret and 2¼" (5.5 cm) from fold of blocked beret edge of I-cord; 31½" (80 cm) circumference at fold and 22" (56 cm) circumference at brim; to fit a woman's large.

Notions: Stitch markers (m); tapestry needle.

Note: Beret can be made larger or smaller by knitting more or fewer rnds of the crown and by working I-cord edge tighter or looser as desired.

115

ALL NEW HOMESPUN HANDKNIT

Thistle

Key

- ☐ MC
- ⊡ CC1
- ⊡ CC2
- ⊟ CC3
- ▣ CC4
- ◉ CC5
- ▨ CC6
- ☐ No stitch
- ⋀ Sl 2, k1, p2sso (MC)
- ⋀ Sl 2, k2, p2sso (CC5)
- ☐ Pattern repeat

CROWN

CO 8 sts. Arrange sts evenly over 4 dpns, place marker (pm), and join for working in the rnd, being careful not to twist sts.

RND 1: [K1 through back loop (tbl)] to end.

RND 2: [K1, M1 (see Glossary)] to end—16 sts.

RNDS 3–5: Knit.

RND 6: [K1, M1] to end—32 sts.

RNDS 7–11: Knit.

RND 12: [K1, M1] to end—64 sts.

RNDS 13–19: Knit.

RND 20: [K2, M1] to end—96 sts.
Continue as established, working inc rnd every 6th rnd and working 1 more st between inc's, two more times.
Knit 5 rnds.

NEXT RND: [K10, M1] to end—176 sts.
Work 5 rnds even.

NEXT RND: K8, [K12, M1] fourteen times—190 sts.

Note: To enlarge or reduce beret size, rep inc rnd more or fewer times to desired number of sts, working more or fewer inc's on last inc rnd for a mult of 10 sts.

THISTLE PATTERN

Work Rnds 1–16 of Thistle chart.

BRIM

RND 1: *K3, k2tog; rep from * to end—152 sts rem.

RND 2: Knit.

RND 3: *K6, k2tog; rep from * to end—133 sts rem.
Work 5-st I-cord BO. Graft ends of I-cord tog.

FINISHING

Block beret on a tam blocker or appropriately sized dinner plate. An occasional light brushing on the outer surface keeps the beret in tip-top shape.

117

glitterpants

{Kathryn Tewson}

These shorties are made with Merino wool for softness and Firestar for strength
and sparkle. Shorties, or soakers, are wool diaper covers, which are becoming popular as more
parents choose cloth diapers for their children. Wool is antibacterial and antimicrobial and,
when treated with lanolin, surprisingly waterproof yet breathable. The lanolin in the wool keeps
these shorties remarkably clean. Over time, the fabric will full slightly, creating an even softer
and more impervious soaker; the wool must not be superwash to work properly.

Spinning Notes

Fiber: 3 oz (85 g) batt (75% Merino top/25%
hand-dyed nylon Firestar).

Drafting method: Long draw.

Wheel system: Double drive.

Ratio: 12:1.

Singles direction spun: Z.

Singles wraps per inch: 9.

Total yardage: 120 yd (110 m).

Yards per pound: 640.

Knitting Notes

Yarn classification: Bulky (Bulky #5).

Yardage used: 73 (81, 90, 99, 109, 120,
132) yd (67 [74, 82, 91, 100, 110, 121] m).

Needles: U.S. size 7 (4.5 mm) and U.S. size
5 (3.75 mm): set of 5 double-pointed (dpn);
16" (40 cm) circular (cir; optional). Adjust
needle size if necessary to obtain the
correct gauge.

Notions: 4 stitch markers (m); tapestry needle;
waste yarn.

Gauge: 20 sts and 28 rows = 4" (10 cm) on
larger needles. Fabric should be firm.

Finished size: 12¾ (14½, 16, 17½,
19¼, 20¾, 22½)" (32.5 [37, 40.5, 44.5,
49, 52.5, 57] cm); to fit a newborn (3, 6, 9,
12, 18, 24 months).

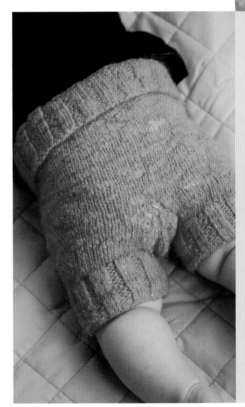

119

Lanolinization

The soaker must be well lanolinized to work properly. To lanolinize the piece, squeeze about 1" (2.5 cm) of Lansinoh (a lanolin-based cream sold in drugstores with supplies for nursing mothers) into a small container. Add about a teaspoon of no-rinse lanolin-enriched wool wash and very hot water to melt the lanolin. Stir to emulsify, and then pour the mixture into a sink or bowl with enough very hot water to cover the soaker completely. Wearing gloves, add the soaker and knead so that the wool wash—lanolin mixture penetrates wool fibers. Squeeze out water and let the soaker dry thoroughly before use. Because the ammonia from the urine reacts with the lanolin to make soap, the soakers will rarely need washing; just rinse them thoroughly and re-lanolinize about once a month.

(Some specialty manufacturers produce liquid lanolin, liquid lanolin spray, and high-lanolin-content wool washes, which can make the lanolinization process a lot easier.)

WAIST

With smaller dpns, CO 64 (72, 80, 88, 96, 104, 112) stitches. Join for working in the rnd, being careful not to twist sts.
Work in [k2, p2] rib for 15 rnds; piece measures about 2" (5 cm).
NEXT RND: Place marker (pm), after 19 (21, 23, 25, 27, 29, 31) sts, after 32 (36, 40, 44, 48, 52, 56) sts, and after 45 (51, 57, 63, 69, 75, 81) sts. Beginning of round is center back of soaker; markers indicate center back, center front, and 3 sts forward of the side point on each hip.

Short-rows

Change to larger needles. Work short-rows (see Glossary) as foll: *Knit to first marker (right hip), wrap and turn. Purl to third marker (left hip), wrap and turn. Knit back to the center back marker. This completes one short-row.
Work in St st for 4 rnds.
Rep from * until front of the piece measures 4¼ (5¼, 5¾, 6¼, 7, 7½, 8)" (11 [13.5, 14.5, 16, 18, 19, 20.5] cm) long from base of ribbing, ending 1 st before center back marker; move m here for new beg of rnd.

Shape Gusset

Note: Short-row shaping continues as gussets are worked, along with increasing at the back gusset on short-rows. Back of gusset will grow more quickly than front.

RND 1: P2, knit to 1 st before center front marker, pm, p1, remove m, p1, knit to end. *Note:* Purl sts indicate outer edges of gusset; work all inc's just inside purl sts.
RND 2: *P1, [work lifted increase (see Glossary)] twice working into front and back of loop to avoid a hole, p1, knit to

	newborn	3 months	6 months	9 months	12 months	18 months	24 months
Cast-On	64	72	80	88	96	104	112
Marker Placement	0, 19, 32, 45	0, 21, 36, 51	0, 23, 40, 57	0, 25, 44, 63	0, 27, 48, 69	0, 29, 52, 75	0, 31, 56, 81
Body Length	4¾"/12 cm	5¼"/13.5 cm	5¾"/14.5 cm	6¼"/16 cm	7"/18 cm	7½"/19 cm	8"/20.5 cm
Gusset Stitches	16	18	20	22	24	26	28
Short-rows/Body	7	8	9	9	10	11	12
Short-rows/Gusset	2	2	2	3	3	3	3
Stitches In Each Leg	36	40	44	48	52	56	60

center m; rep from * to end of rnd—4 sts inc'd.

RND 3: *P1, M1R (see Glossary), k2, M1L, p1, knit to center m; rep from * to end of rnd—4 sts inc'd.

Continue as established, increasing 4 sts on each rnd and working 2 more sts between incs on each rnd, for every rnd and every short-row (including purl rows), until there are 20 (22, 24, 28, 30, 32, 34) knit sts between purl sts at back of soaker. Discontinue short-rows.

NEXT RND: (dec rnd) P1, k2tog, k to 3 sts before next marker, ssk, p1, work to end and at the same time inc at front of the gusset.

Continue to dec at back of gusset and inc at front of gusset until there are 16 (18, 20, 22, 24, 26, 28) sts between purl sts at both front and back.

Divide Legs

Knit to beg of front gusset, transfer 32 (36, 40, 44, 48, 52, 56) right leg sts (including purl border sts) onto waste yarn, sl 16 (18, 20, 22, 24, 26, 28) front gusset sts onto 1 dpn, transfer 32 (36, 40, 44, 48, 52, 56) left leg sts to waste yarn, sl 16 (18, 20, 22, 24, 26, 28) back gusset sts to another

dpn. Graft front and back of gusset using Kitchener st (see Glossary).

Arrange right leg sts on 4 smaller dpns and pick up and knit (see Glossary) 4 sts along gusset edge—36 (40, 44, 48, 52, 56, 60) sts. Work [k2, p2] rib for 15 rnds. BO loosely in patt. Rep for left leg. Weave in ends.

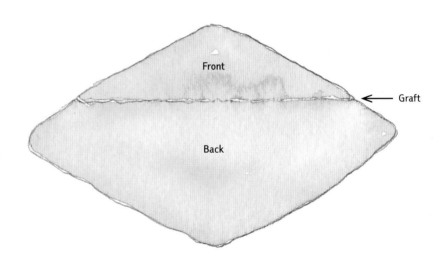

Front

Back

Graft

entrelac socks

{Erda Kappeler}

Entrelac is a wonderful way to use a variety of yarns, and it can be addictive. These socks combine small amounts of six different-colored yarns with a heathered main color that ties them together. The cuffs are an excellent place to blend different yarns with the same grist—try a fluffy angora or shiny Tencel blend for some of the entrelac squares. These socks are a great opportunity to practice knitting backward; it may help to look in the mirror while practicing until you've got the hang of it.

Spinning Notes

Fiber: 5 oz (142 g) superwash Merino (2 oz [57 g] of MC and ½ oz [14 g] of each of 6 colors).

Shown here: 2 oz (57 g) dark blue (MC) from Ashland Bay; ½ oz (14 g) in Kelly green, ½ oz (14 g) teal, ½ oz (14 g) blue, ½ oz (14 g) turquoise, ½ oz (14 g) purple, and ½ oz (14 g) gray (all hand-dyed).

Drafting method: Long draw over the fold.

Wheel system: Double drive.

Ratio (singles/plying): 10:1 (singles), 13:1 (plying).

Singles direction spun: Z.

Number of plies: 2.

Plied direction spun: S.

Plied twists per inch: 4.5.

Plied wraps per inch: 14.

Total yardage: 277 yd (253 m).

Yards per pound: 866.

Knitting Notes

Yarn classification: Fingering weight (Super Fine #1).

Yardage used: 160 yd [146 m].

Needles: U.S. size 3 (3.25 mm): set of 5 double-pointed (dpn). Adjust needle size if necessary to obtain the correct gauge.

Notions: Waste yarn (for afterthought heel); stitch markers (m); sewing thread (to reinforce heel); tapestry needle.

Gauge: 14 sts and 20 rnds = 2" (5 cm) in St st.

Finished size: 8" (20.5 cm) cuff and 9½" (24 cm) from back of heel to toe; to fit a woman's size 9.

123

CUFF

With Kelly green, CO 42 sts. Join for working in the rnd, being careful not to twist sts.

RNDS 1–6: With Kelly green, knit.
RNDS 7–10: *With gray, k1, with Kelly green, k1; rep from * to end.
RND 11: With gray, knit.
RND 12: With gray, k4 [k2tog, k8] three times, k2tog, k4—36 sts rem.

ENTRELAC

Start by knitting a row of triangles to form the base for the entrelac, then pick up and knit sts (see Glossary) along the edges of the triangles to form rectangles.

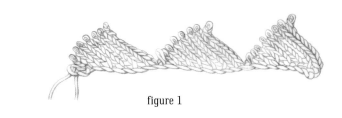

figure 1

Foundation Triangles
first triangles (figure 1)

ROW 1: With purple, k2, turn.
ROW 2: Sl 1, p1, turn.
ROW 3: Sl 1, k2, turn.
ROW 4: Sl 1, p2, turn.
ROW 5: Sl 1, k3, turn.
ROW 6: Sl 1, p3, turn.
ROW 7: Sl 1, k4, turn.
ROW 8: Sl 1, p4, turn.
ROW 9: Sl 1, k5. Do not turn.
Rep Rows 1–9 five more times.

right-leaning rectangle (R-rec)

For the first row of rectangles, work around the sock in the opposite direction, picking up sts from the right sides of the triangles and knitting live sts from the triangles tog with the last st from the rectangle sts (Figure 2).

   *With MC and WS facing, pick up and purl (see Glossary) 5 sts along right edge of first triangle (which will appear as the left edge from WS), pick up and purl 1 st between first and last triangles, p1 from last triangle—7 sts.

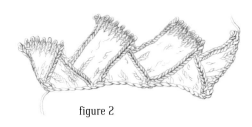

figure 2

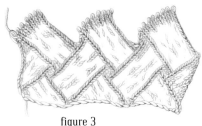

figure 3

ROW 1: K2tog, k5, turn—6 sts rem.
ROW 2: Sl 1, p5, slip last st from triangle to left needle, turn—7 sts.
Rep Rows 1–2 until all sts from last triangle have been worked—6 sts rem. Turn work. Rep from * five more times.

   With 6 sts from R-rec on needle, break yarn and weave in end.

left-leaning rectangle (L-rec)

For the second row of rectangles, pick up sts from the left sides of the rectangles (Figure 2).

*With blue and RS facing, pick up and knit 5 sts along left edge of L-rec, pick up and knit 1 st between first and last R-rec, k1 from last R-rec—7 sts.

ROW 1: Sl 1, p5, turn
ROW 2: Sl 1, k4, sl last st kwise, sl next st from R-rec kwise, then k2 sl sts tog tbl, turn—6 sts.

Rep Rows 1–2 until all sts from last rectangle have been worked—6 sts rem.
   Rep from * five times.

rectangle rounds 3–5

With MC, work one rnd of R-rec. With teal, work one rnd of L-rec. With MC, work 1 rnd of R-rec.

triangles

*With turquoise and RS facing pick up and knit 5 sts along left edge R-rec, k1 from next R-rec.

ROW 1: Sl 1, p1, turn—2 sts.
ROW 2: Sl 1, k2, turn—3 sts.
ROW 3: Sl 1, p3, turn—4 sts.
ROW 4: Sl 1, k4, turn—5 sts.
ROW 5: Sl 1, p5, turn—6 sts.
ROW 6: Sl 1, k6, turn—7 sts.
ROW 7: Sl 1, p6, p2tog from R-rec, turn—8 sts.

ROW 8: Sl 1, k6, k2tog from next R-rec—
8 sts.

Rep from * five more times—54 sts.

NEXT ROW: (dec row) K6, [k2tog, k11] three
times, k2tog, k7—50 sts.

Foot

RNDS 1–3: With MC, knit.

RND 4: (heel rnd) With waste yarn, k25 sts,
sl 25 sts back to left needle; with MC, knit
to end of rnd.

RNDS 5–7: With MC, knit.

RNDS 8–10: With Kelly green, knit.

RNDS 11–13: *With MC, k1, with Kelly
green, k1; rep from * to end.

RNDS 14–19: With MC, knit.

Rep Rnds 5–19 two more times, then rep
Rnds 5–13 one more time, or to desired
length from back of heel to base of toes.

Toe

RND 1: Place marker (pm), with MC, k25,
pm, knit to end.

RNDS 2–12: Ssk, knit to 2 sts before
m, k2tog, ssk, knit to 2 sts before m,
k2tog—4 sts dec'd; 6 sts rem after
Rnd 12.

RND 13: Ssk, k1, k2tog, k1—4 sts rem.

RND 14: Ssk, k2tog—2 sts rem.

RND 15: K2tog.

Cut yarn. Draw tail through rem st to
secure and fasten off on WS.

Heel

Remove waste yarn from heel, arranging
50 revealed sts evenly over 4 dpns.

RND 1: Pm, with MC, k25, pm, knit to end.

RND 2: Ssk, knit to 2 sts before m, k2tog,
ssk, knit to 2 sts before m, k2tog—4
sts dec'd.

RND 3: Knit.

Rep Rnds 2–3 eight more times—14 sts
rem.

Using three-needle method (see
Glossary), BO rem sts.

FINISHING

Weave in ends. Roll the socks up in a thick
towel, being careful to avoid wrinkling the
socks. Place the towel and socks inside
a plastic bag. Wet the towel and socks
well and leave to soak for several hours.
Remove socks from bag and towel and lay
flat to dry on a fresh towel.

125

happy headband

{Liz Gipson}

For Liz Gipson, welcoming four cashmere-bearing goats into her backyard also meant welcoming cashmere fiber onto her needles. This headband uses her first ounces of precious handspun cashmere in a warm and soft lace headband perfect for chilly mornings. Concerned that the weight of the spindle would break the delicate yarn, she began spinning the yarn on a supported spindle but soon found that the twist held the fibers together firmly. The twist in the headband allows it to snug to the base of your neck and create less bulk.

Spinning Notes

Fiber: 1 oz (28 g) cashmere top.
Drafting method: Short draw.
Spindle: 1½ oz (43 g) supported spindle.
Singles direction spun: Z.
Singles wraps per inch: 40.
Number of plies: 2.
Plied direction spun: S.
Plied twists per inch: 11.
Plied wraps per inch: 20.
Total yardage: 74 yd (68 m).
Yards per pound: 1,184.

Knitting Notes

Yarn classification: Laceweight (Lace #0).
Yardage used: 58 yd (53 m).
Needles: U.S. size 6 (4.0 mm). Adjust needle size if necessary to obtain the correct gauge.
Notions: Tapestry needle.
Gauge: 14 sts and 16 rows = 2" (5 cm).
Finished size: 4" (10 cm) wide and 21" (53.5 cm) head circumference.

127

 stitch guide St. John's Wort Lace pattern

(multiple of 6 sts + 2)

(from *Traditional Knitted Lace Shawls* by Martha Waterman, Interweave, 1998)

ROW 1: K1, *sl 1, k2, psso, k3; rep from * to last st, k1.

ROW 2: P1, *p1, yo, p4; rep from * to last st, p1.

ROW 3: K1, *k3, sl 1, k2, psso; rep from * to last st, end k1.

ROW 4: P1, *p4, yo, p1; rep from * to last st, p1.

Rep Rows 1–4 for patt.

Note: It is easy to find your place in the pattern by noting that on even-numbered rows the yo falls between the k2 sts over which the slipped sts have been passed.

HEADBAND

Using crochet provisional method (see Glossary), CO 38 sts.

Work in St. John's Wort Lace patt for 21" (53.5 cm).

FINISHING

Twist one end of the work for a full rotation. Unzip crochet chain CO and place revealed sts on a needle facing the same direction as the needle holding the last row. Keeping twist in place, use the Kitchener st (see Glossary) to graft the ends together.

abbreviations

beg(s)	begin(s); beginning		**rev St st**	reverse stockinette stitch
BO	bind off		**rnd(s)**	round(s)
CC	contrasting color		**RS**	right side
cm	centimeter(s)		**sl**	slip
cn	cable needle		**sl st**	slip st (slip 1 stitch purlwise unless otherwise indicated)
CO	cast on		**ssk**	slip 2 stitches knitwise, one at a time, from the left needle to right needle, insert left needle tip through both front loops and knit together from this position (1 stitch decrease)
cont	continue(s); continuing			
dec(s)	decrease(s); decreasing			
dpn	double-pointed needles			
foll	follow(s); following			
g	gram(s)			
inc(s)	increase(s); increasing		**st(s)**	stitch(es)
k	knit		**St st**	stockinette stitch
k1f&b	knit into the front and back of same stitch		**tbl**	through back loop
			tog	together
kwise	knitwise, as if to knit		**WS**	wrong side
m	marker(s)		**wyb**	with yarn in back
MC	main color		**wyf**	with yarn in front
mm	millimeter(s)		**yd**	yard(s)
M1	make one (increase)		**yo**	yarnover
p	purl		*****	repeat starting point
p1f&b	purl into front and back of same stitch		*** ***	repeat all instructions between asterisks
			( )	alternate measurements and/or instructions
patt(s)	pattern(s)			
psso	pass slipped stitch over		**[ ]**	work instructions as a group a specified number of times
pwise	purlwise, as if to purl			
rem	remain(s); remaining			
rep	repeat(s); repeating			

glossary

BIND-OFFS
I-Cord Bind-Off

With right side facing and using the knitted method (see page 131), cast on 3 stitches (for cord) onto the end of the needle holding the stitches to be bound off **(Figure 1)**, *k2, k2tog through back loops (the last cord stitch with the first stitch to be bound off; **Figure 2**), slip these 3 stitches back to the left needle **(Figure 3)**, and pull the yarn firmly from the back. Repeat from * until 3 stitches remain on left needle and no stitches remain on right needle. Bind off remaining stitches using the standard method (below).

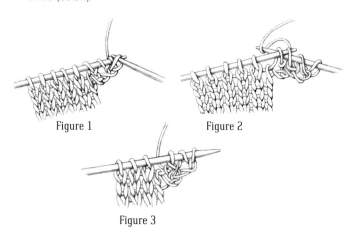

Figure 1   Figure 2

Figure 3

Standard Bind-Off

Knit the first stitch, *knit the next stitch (2 stitches on right needle), insert left needle tip into first stitch on right needle **(Figure 1)** and lift this stitch up and over the second stitch **(Figure 2)** and off the needle **(Figure 3)**. Repeat from * for the desired number of stitches.

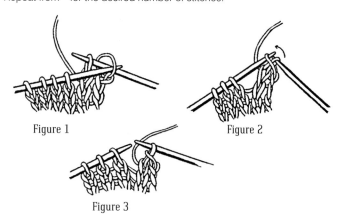

Figure 1   Figure 2

Figure 3

Three-Needle Bind-Off

Place the stitches to be joined onto two separate needles and hold the needles parallel so that the right sides of knitting face together. Insert a third needle into the first stitch on each of two needles **(Figure 1)** and knit them together as 1 stitch **(Figure 2)**, *knit the next stitch on each needle the same way, then use the left needle tip to lift the first stitch over the second and off the needle **(Figure 3)**. Repeat from * until no stitches remain on first two needles. Cut yarn and pull tail through last stitch to secure.

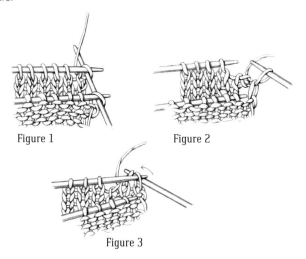

Figure 1   Figure 2

Figure 3

CAST-ONS
Backward-Loop Cast-On

*Loop working yarn and place it on needle backward so that it doesn't unwind. Repeat from *.

Cable Cast-On

If there are no stitches on the needles, make a slipknot of working yarn and place it on the needle, then use the knitted method to cast on one more stitch—2 stitches on needle. Hold needle with working yarn in your left hand with the wrong side of the work facing you. *Insert right needle between the first 2 stitches on left needle **(Figure 1)**, wrap yarn around needle as if to knit, draw yarn through **(Figure 2)**, and place new loop on left needle **(Figure 3)** to form a new stitch. Repeat from * for the desired number of stitches, always working between the first 2 stitches on the left needle.

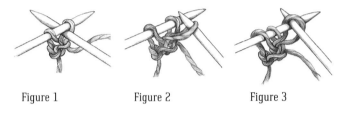

Figure 1   Figure 2   Figure 3

Crochet Chain Provisional Cast-On

With waste yarn and crochet hook, make a loose crochet chain (see page 132) about 4 stitches more than you need to cast on. With knitting needle, working yarn, and beginning 2 stitches from end of chain, pick up and knit 1 stitch through the back loop of each crochet chain **(Figure 1)** for desired number of stitches. When you're ready to work in the opposite direction, pull out the crochet chain to expose live stitches **(Figure 2)**.

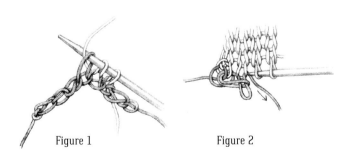

Figure 1   Figure 2

Invisible Provisional Cast-On

Make a loose slipknot of working yarn and place it on the right needle. Hold a length of contrasting waste yarn next to the slipknot and around your left thumb; hold working yarn over your left index finger. *Bring the right needle forward, then under waste yarn, over working yarn, grab a loop of working yarn and bring it forward under working yarn **(Figure 1)**, then bring needle back behind the working yarn and grab a second loop **(Figure 2)**. Repeat from * for the desired number of stitches. When you're ready to work in the opposite direction, place the exposed loops on a knitting needle as you pull out the waste yarn.

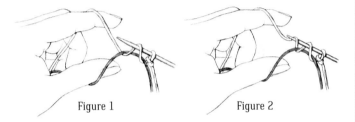

Figure 1   Figure 2

Knitted Cast-On

Make a slipknot of working yarn and place it on the left needle if there are no stitches already there. *Use the right needle to knit the first stitch (or slipknot) on left needle **(Figure 1)** and place new loop onto left needle to form a new stitch **(Figure 2)**. Repeat from * for the desired number of stitches, always working into the last stitch made.

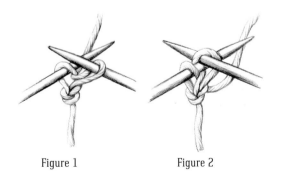

Figure 1   Figure 2

131

glossary {continued}

Long-Tail (Continental) Cast-On

Leaving a long tail (about ½" [1.3 cm] for each stitch to be cast on), make a slipknot and place on right needle. Place thumb and index finger of your left hand between the yarn ends so that working yarn is around your index finger and tail end is around your thumb and secure the yarn ends with your other fingers. Hold your palm upward, making a V of yarn **(Figure 1)**. *Bring needle up through loop on thumb **(Figure 2)**, catch first strand around index finger, and go back down through loop on thumb **(Figure 3)**. Drop loop off thumb and, placing thumb back in V configuration, tighten resulting stitch on needle **(Figure 4)**. Repeat from * for the desired number of stitches.

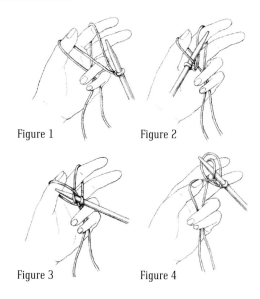

Figure 1   Figure 2

Figure 3   Figure 4

COLOR
Intarsia

When working intarsia (sometimes called "picture knitting"), a separate strand of yarn is generally used for each color. Twist the old color around the new color at each color change to prevent holes from forming at the joins.

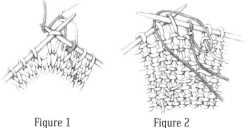

Figure 1   Figure 2

CROCHET
Crochet Chain (ch)

Make a slipknot and place it on crochet hook if there isn't a loop already on the hook. *Yarn over hook and draw through loop on hook. Repeat from * for the desired number of stitches. To fasten off, cut yarn and draw end through last loop formed.

Single Crochet (sc)

*Insert hook into the second chain from the hook (or the next stitch), yarn over hook and draw through a loop, yarn over hook **(Figure 1)**, and draw it through both loops on hook **(Figure 2)**. Repeat from * for the desired number of stitches.

Figure 1   Figure 2

Slip-Stitch Crochet (sl st)

*Insert hook into stitch, yarn over hook and draw a loop through both the stitch and the loop already on hook. Repeat from * for the desired number of stitches.

DECREASES
Knit 2 Together (k2tog)

Knit 2 stitches together as if they were a single stitch.

Knit 3 Together (k3tog)

Knit 3 stitches together as if they were a single stitch.

Purl 2 Together (p2tog)

Purl 2 stitches together as if they were a single stitch.

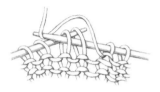

Slip, Slip, Knit (ssk)

Slip 2 stitches individually knitwise (**Figure 1**), insert left needle tip into the front of these 2 slipped stitches, and use the right needle to knit them together through their back loops (**Figure 2**).

Figure 1   Figure 2

Slip, Slip, Purl (ssp)

Holding yarn in front, slip 2 stitches individually knitwise (**Figure 1**), then slip these 2 stitches back onto left needle (they will be turned on the needle) and purl them together through their back loops (**Figure 2**).

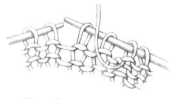

Figure 1   Figure 2

Slip, Slip, Slip, Knit (sssk)

Slip 3 stitches individually knitwise, insert left needle tip into the front of these 3 slipped stitches, and use the right needle to knit them together through their back loops.

Slip, Slip, Slip, Purl (sssp)

Holding yarn in front, slip 3 stitches individually knitwise, then slip these 3 stitches back onto left needle (they will be turned on the needle) and purl them together through their back loops.

EMBROIDERY
Buttonhole Stitch

Working into the edge half-stitch of the knitted piece, *bring tip of threaded needle in and out of a knitted stitch, place working yarn under needle tip, then bring threaded needle through the stitch and tighten. Repeat from *, always bringing threaded needle on top of working yarn.

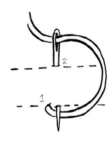

Straight Stitch

*Bring threaded needle out of knitted background from back to front at the base of the stitches to be covered, then in from front to back at the tip of the stitches to be covered). Repeat from *, working in straight lines or radiating from a point as desired.

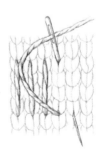

glossary {continued}

Duplicate Stitch

Diagonal: Bring threaded needle out from back to front at the base of the V of the knitted stitch you want to cover. Working right to left, *pass needle in and out under the stitch in the row above it and back into the base of the same stitch. Bring needle back out at the base of the V in the next stitch to be covered. Repeat from * for the desired number of stitches.

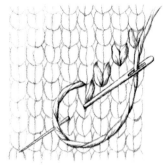

Horizontal: Bring threaded needle out from back to front at the base of the V of the knitted stitch you want to cover. *Working right to left, pass needle in and out under the stitch in the row above it and back into the base of the same stitch. Bring needle back out at the base of the V of the next stitch to the left. Repeat from * for desired number of stitches.

Vertical: Beginning at lowest point, work as for horizontal duplicate stitch, ending by bringing the needle back out at the base of the stitch directly above the stitch just worked.

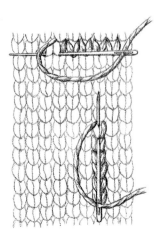

GRAFTING
Kitchener Stitch

Arrange stitches on two needles so that there is the same number of stitches on each needle. Hold the needles parallel to each other with wrong sides of the knitting together. Allowing about ½" (1.3 cm) per stitch to be grafted, thread matching yarn on a tapestry needle. Work from right to left as follows:

Step 1. Bring tapestry needle through the first stitch on the front needle as if to purl and leave the stitch on the needle **(Figure 1)**.

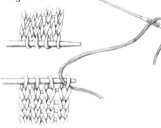

Figure 1

Step 2. Bring tapestry needle through the first stitch on the back needle as if to knit and leave that stitch on the needle **(Figure 2)**.

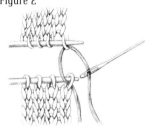

Figure 2

Step 3. Bring tapestry needle through the first front stitch as if to knit and slip this stitch off the needle, then bring tapestry needle through the next front stitch as if to purl and leave this stitch on the needle **(Figure 3)**.

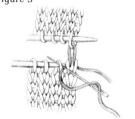

Figure 3

Step 4. Bring tapestry needle through the first back stitch as if to purl and slip this stitch off the needle, then bring tapestry needle through the next back stitch as if to knit and leave this stitch on the needle **(Figure 4)**.

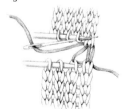

Figure 4

Repeat Steps 3 and 4 until 1 stitch remains on each needle, adjusting the tension to match the rest of the knitting as you go. To finish, bring tapestry needle through the front stitch as if to knit and slip this stitch off the needle, then bring tapestry needle through the back stitch as if to purl and slip this stitch off the needle.

134

I-CORD

Using two double-pointed needles, cast on the desired number of stitches (usually 3 to 4). *Without turning the needle, slide stitches to other end of needle, pull the yarn around the back, and knit the stitches as usual. Repeat from * for desired length.

Applied I-Cord: As I-cord is knitted, attach it to the garment as follows:
With garment right side facing and using a separate ball of yarn and circular needle, pick up and knit the desired number of stitches along the garment edge. Slide these stitches down the needle so that the first picked-up stitch is near the opposite needle point. With double-pointed needle, cast on the desired number of I-cord stitches. *Knit across the I-cord to the last stitch, then knit the last stitch together with the first picked-up stitch on the garment, and pull the yarn behind the cord. Repeat from * until all picked-up stitches have been used.

INCREASES

Bar Increase (k1f&b)

Knit into a stitch but leave it on the left needle **(Figure 1)**, then knit through the back loop of the same stitch **(Figure 2)** and slip the original stitch off the needle **(Figure 3)**.

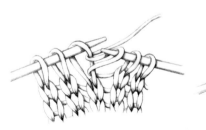

Figure 1

Figure 2

Figure 3

Lifted Increase—Left Slant

Insert left needle tip into the back of the stitch below the stitch just knitted **(Figure 1)**, then knit this stitch **(Figure 2)**.

Figure 1

Figure 2

Lifted Increase—Right Slant

Note: If no slant direction is specified, use the right slant.
Knit into the back of the stitch (in the "purl bump") in the row directly below the stitch on the needle **(Figure 1)**, then knit the stitch on the needle **(Figure 2)**, and slip the original stitch off the needle.

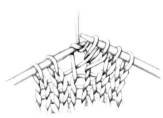

Figure 1

Figure 2

Raised Make One—Left Slant (M1L)

Note: Use the left slant if no direction of slant is specified.
With left needle tip, lift the strand between the last knitted stitch and the first stitch on the left needle from front to back **(Figure 1)**, then knit the lifted loop through the back **(Figure 2)**.

Figure 1

Figure 2

135

glossary {continued}

P1f&b

Purl into a stitch but leave it on the left needle **(Figure 1)**, then purl through the back loop of the same stitch **(Figure 2)** and slip the original stitch off the needle.

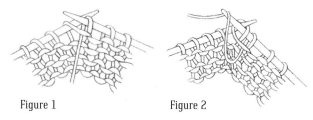

Figure 1   Figure 2

Raised Make One Purlwise (M1 pwise)

With left needle tip, lift the strand between the needles from back to front **(Figure 1)**, then purl the lifted loop through the front **(Figure 2)**.

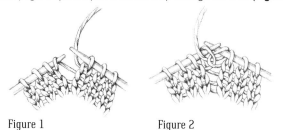

Figure 1   Figure 2

Raised Make One—Right Slant (M1R)

With left needle tip, lift the strand between the needles from back to front **(Figure 1)**. Knit the lifted loop through the front **(Figure 2)**.

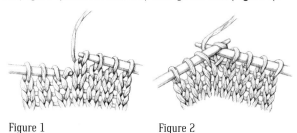

Figure 1   Figure 2

Yarnover

Wrap the working yarn around the needle from front to back and in position to knit the next stitch.

PICK UP AND KNIT
Pick Up and Knit Along CO or BO Edge

With right side facing and working from right to left, insert the tip of the needle into the center of the stitch below the bind-off or cast-on edge **(Figure 1)**, wrap yarn around needle, and pull through a loop **(Figure 2)**. Pick up one stitch for every existing stitch.

Figure 1   Figure 2

Pick Up and Knit Along Shaped Edge

With right side facing and working from right to left, insert tip of needle between last and second-to-last stitches, wrap yarn around needle, and pull through a loop. Pick up and knit about 3 stitches for every four rows, adjusting as necessary so that picked-up edge lays flat.

Pick Up and Knit Back Loop, Both Loops, and Front Loop

With right sides facing and working from right to left, insert tip of needle under the front half **(Figure 1)** or both halves **(Figure 2)** of stitch along selvedge edge, wrap yarn around needle, and pull it through to form a stitch on the needle. For a tighter join, pick up the stitches and knit them through the back loop **(Figure 3)**.

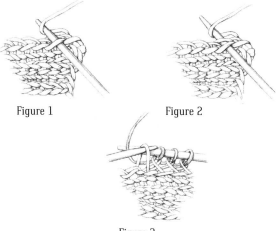

Figure 1   Figure 2

Figure 3

ALL NEW HOMESPUN HANDKNIT

Pick Up and Purl

With wrong side of work facing and working from right to left, *insert needle tip under selvedge stitch from the far side to the near side, wrap yarn around needle **(Figure 1)**, and pull a loop through **(Figure 2)**. Repeat from * for desired number of stitches.

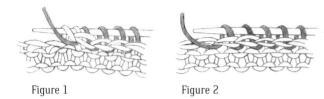

Figure 1   Figure 2

POM-POM

Cut two circles of cardboard, each ½" (1.3 cm) larger than desired finished pom-pom width. Cut a small circle out of the center and a small wedge out of the side of each circle **(Figure 1)**. Tie a strand of yarn between the circles, hold circles together and wrap with yarn—the more wraps, the thicker the pom-pom. Cut between the circles and knot the tie strand tightly (Figure 2). Place pom-pom between two smaller cardboard circles held together with a needle and trim the edges **(Figure 3)**. This technique comes from Nicky Epstein's *Knitted Embellishments*, Interweave, 1999.

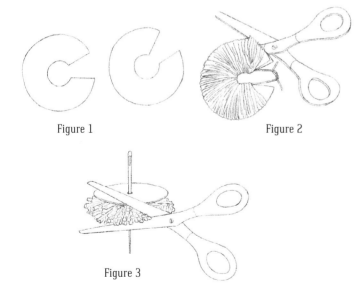

Figure 1   Figure 2

Figure 3

SEAMS

Backstitch Seam—Horizontal

Pin pieces to be seamed with right sides facing together. Working from right to left into the stitch just below the bind-off row, bring threaded needle up between the first 2 stitches on each piece of knitted fabric, then back down through both layers, 1 stitch to the right of the starting point **(Figure 1)**. *Bring the needle up through both layers a stitch to the left of the backstitch just made **(Figure 2)**, then back down to the right, through the same hole used before **(Figure 3)**. Repeat from *, working backward 1 stitch for every 2 stitches worked forward.

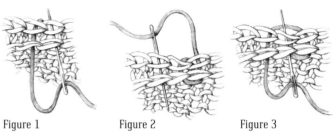

Figure 1   Figure 2   Figure 3

Invisible Horizontal Seam

Working with the bound-off edges opposite each other, right sides of the knitting facing you, and working into the stitches just below the bound-off edges, bring threaded tapestry needle out at the center of the first stitch (i.e., go under half of the first stitch) on one side of the seam, then bring needle in and out under the first whole stitch on the other side **(Figure 1)**. *Bring needle into the center of the same stitch it came out of before, then out in the center of the adjacent stitch **(Figure 2)**. Bring needle in and out under the next whole stitch on the other side **(Figure 3)**. Repeat from *, ending with a half-stitch on the first side.

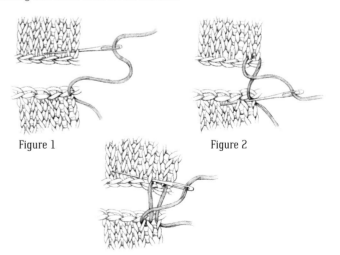

Figure 1   Figure 2

Figure 3

137

glossary {continued}

Invisible Vertical to Horizontal Seam

With yarn threaded on a tapestry needle, pick up 1 bar between the first 2 stitches along the vertical edge **(Figure 1)**, then pick up 1 complete stitch along the horizontal edge **(Figure 2)**. *Pick up the next 1 or 2 bars on the first piece, then the next whole stitch on the other piece **(Figure 3)**. Repeat from *, ending by picking up 1 bar on the vertical edge.

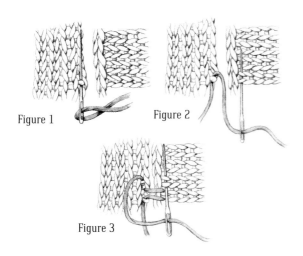

Figure 1

Figure 2

Figure 3

Mattress Stitch

Insert threaded needle under 1 bar between the 2 edge stitches on one piece **(Figure 1)**, then under the corresponding bar plus the bar above it on the other piece **(Figure 2)**. *Pick up the next 2 bars on the first piece **(Figure 3)**, then the 2 two bars on the other. Repeat from *, ending by picking up the last bar or pair of bars on the first piece. To reduce bulk in the mattress-stitch seam, work as for the 1-stitch seam allowance but pick up the bars in the center of the edge stitches instead of between the last 2 stitches.

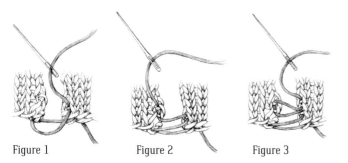

Figure 1

Figure 2

Figure 3

Garter Stitch

Insert threaded needle under the lower purl bar between the 2 edge stitches on one piece **(Figure 1)**, then the upper purl bar from the stitch next to the edge stitch on the same row of the other piece **(Figure 2)**.

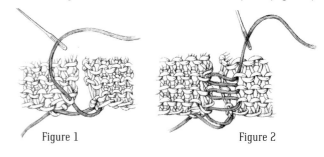

Figure 1

Figure 2

Slip-Stitch Crochet Seam

With right sides together and working 1 stitch at a time, *insert crochet hook through both thicknesses into the stitch just below the bound-off edge (or 1 stitch in from the selvedge edge), grab a loop of yarn **(Figure 1)**, and draw this loop through both thicknesses, then through the loop on the hook **(Figure 2)**. Repeat from *, keeping even tension on the crochet stitches.

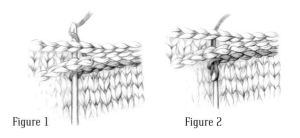

Figure 1

Figure 2

Whipstitch

Hold pieces to be sewn together so that the edges to be seamed are even with each other. With yarn threaded on a tapestry needle, *insert needle through both layers from back to front, then bring needle to back. Repeat from *, keeping even tension on the seaming yarn.

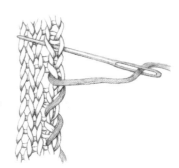

SHORT-ROWS
Short-Rows Knit Side

Work to turning point, slip next stitch purlwise **(Figure 1)**, bring the yarn to the front, then slip the same stitch back to the left needle **(Figure 2)**, turn the work around and bring the yarn in position for the next stitch—1 stitch has been wrapped and the yarn is correctly positioned to work the next stitch. When you come to a wrapped stitch on a subsequent row, hide the wrap by working it together with the wrapped stitch as follows: Insert right needle tip under the wrap (from the front if wrapped stitch is a knit stitch; from the back if wrapped stitch is a purl stitch; **Figure 3**), then into the stitch on the needle, and work the stitch and its wrap together as a single stitch.

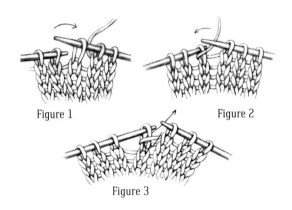

Figure 1   Figure 2

Figure 3

Short-Rows Purl Side

Work to the turning point, slip the next stitch purlwise to the right needle, bring the yarn to the back of the work **(Figure 1)**, return the slipped stitch to the left needle, bring the yarn to the front between the needles **(Figure 2)**, and turn the work so that the knit side is facing—1 stitch has been wrapped and the yarn is correctly positioned to knit the next stitch. To hide the wrap on a subsequent purl row, work to the wrapped stitch, use the tip of the right needle to pick up the wrap from the back, place it on the left needle **(Figure 3)**, then purl it together with the wrapped stitch.

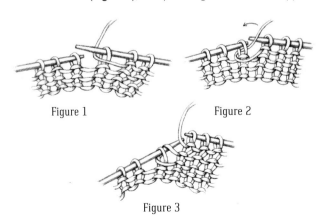

Figure 1   Figure 2

Figure 3

TASSEL

Cut a piece of cardboard 4" (10 cm) wide by the desired length of the tassel plus 1" (2.5 cm). Wrap yarn to desired thickness around cardboard. Cut a short length of yarn and tie tightly around one end of wrapped yarn **(Figure 1)**. Cut yarn loops at other end. Cut another piece of yarn and wrap tightly around loops a short distance below top knot to form tassel neck. Knot securely, thread ends onto tapestry needle, and pull to center of tassel **(Figure 2)**. Trim ends.

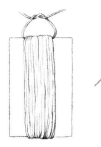

Figure 1   Figure 2

TWISTED CORD

Cut several lengths of yarn about five times the desired finished cord length. Fold the strands in half to form two equal groups. Anchor the strands at the fold by looping them over a doorknob. Holding one group in each hand, twist each group tightly in a clockwise direction until they begin to kink. Put both groups in one hand, then release them, allowing them to twist around each other counterclockwise. Smooth out the twists so that they are uniform along the length of the cord. Knot the ends.

Figure 1   Figure 2

ZIPPER

With right side facing and zipper closed, pin zipper to the knitted pieces so edges cover the zipper teeth. With contrasting thread and right side facing, baste zipper in place close to teeth **(Figure 1)**. Turn work over and with matching sewing thread and needle, stitch outer edges of zipper to wrong side of knitting **(Figure 2)**, being careful to follow a single column of stitches in the knitting to keep zipper straight. Turn work back to right side facing, and with matching sewing thread, sew knitted fabric close to teeth **(Figure 3)**. Remove basting.

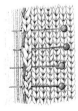

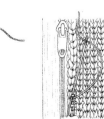

Figure 1   Figure 2   Figure 3

spinning information

Short draw: With your hands close together, draft fibers forward, keeping the drafting triangle a little longer than the staple (**Figures 1a and 1b**).

Long draw: Draw back with fiber supply hand to attenuate the fiber while controlling the twist with the other hand. Feed entire length of yarn onto bobbin in one motion (**Figure 2**).

Medium backward draw: With your forward hand, pinch the yarn just above the drafting triangle. As twist builds up, draw the fiber supply hand back about half the length of the staple. Release the forward hand and allow the twist to move into the drafted fibers.

Spinning from the fold: Fold a length of fiber over the forefinger of your back hand or hold the folded fiber lightly between your thumb and forefinger. Draft from the center of the staple (**Figure 3**).

Spinning from the end: Pull out a few fibers at a time and allow the twist to run up into them. Do not allow the twist to run past these fibers.

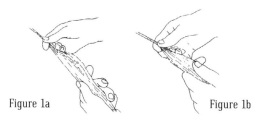

Figure 1a   Figure 1b

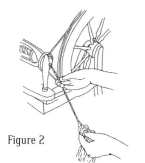

Figure 2

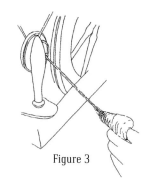

Figure 3

Project Yarns

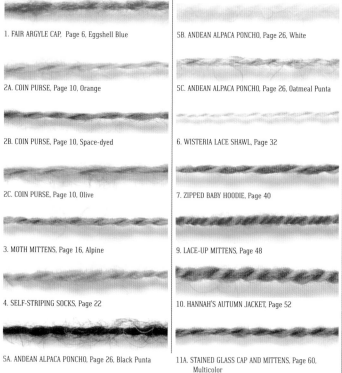

1. FAIR ARGYLE CAP, Page 6, Eggshell Blue

2A. COIN PURSE, Page 10, Orange

2B. COIN PURSE, Page 10, Space-dyed

2C. COIN PURSE, Page 10, Olive

3. MOTH MITTENS, Page 16, Alpine

4. SELF-STRIPING SOCKS, Page 22

5A. ANDEAN ALPACA PONCHO, Page 26, Black Punta

5B. ANDEAN ALPACA PONCHO, Page 26, White

5C. ANDEAN ALPACA PONCHO, Page 26, Oatmeal Punta

6. WISTERIA LACE SHAWL, Page 32

7. ZIPPED BABY HOODIE, Page 40

9. LACE-UP MITTENS, Page 48

10. HANNAH'S AUTUMN JACKET, Page 52

11A. STAINED GLASS CAP AND MITTENS, Page 60, Multicolor

11B. STAINED GLASS CAP AND MITTENS, Page 60, White

12A. NOMAD BAG, Page 64, White

12B. NOMAD BAG, Page 64, Red

12C. NOMAD BAG, Page 64, Yellow

13. DIAMONDS AND PEARLS LACE MITTS, Page 70

14. SPIDER HAT, Page 76, MC

15. OLD GARDEN SCARF, Page 80

16A. CHILD'S NORDIC SET, Page 90, Red

16B. CHILD'S NORDIC SET, Page 90, Oatmeal

16C. CHILD'S NORDIC SET, Page 90, Brown

17A. SHEEPY MITTENS, Page 102, White

17B. SHEEPY MITTENS, Page 102, Gray

17C. SHEEPY MITTENS, Page 102, Brown

18. CHUTES AND LADDERS HAT, Page 106

19A. INDIGO AND LICHEN BERET, Page 114, MC

19B. INDIGO AND LICHEN BERET, Page 114, CC

fiber sources

Ashland Bay Trading Company
11782 SE Jennifer St.
Clackamas, OR 97015
(800) 213-0628
ashlandbay.com

Bountiful
(970) 482-7746
bountifulspinweave.com

Chameleon Colorworks
chameleoncolorworks.com

Decadent Fibers
decadentfibers.com

The Fold
3316 Millstream Rd.
Marengo, IL 60152
(815) 568-5730
thefoldatmc.com

Fox Fibre
Vreseis Limited
PO Box 69
Guinda, CA 95637
(530) 796-3007
vreseis.com

Franquemont Fibers
abbysyarns.com

Kai Ranch Mohair
Route 1
Box 293-C
Lexington, TX 78947
(512) 273-2709

Keepers Farm
Jackie Webb
Cooks Pond Rd.
Milland
Hampshire, England
GU30 7JY
llanwenog.org

Little Barn Inc.
littlebarninc.com

Louet North America
3425 Hands Rd.
Prescott, ON
Canada K0E 1T0
(800) 897-6444
louet.com

The Mannings
1132 Green Ridge Rd.
PO Box 687
East Berlin, PA 17316
(800) 233-7166
the-mannings.com

Morro Fleece Works
1920 Main St.
Morro Bay, CA 93442
(805) 772-9665
morrofleeceworks.com

Rovings
Box 28, Grp 30, RR #1
Dugald, MB
Canada R0E 0K0
(800) 266-5536
rovings.com

The Spinning Loft
123 Mason Rd.
Howell, MI 48843
(517) 540-1344
thespinningloft.com

Spunky Eclectic
33 Webster Rd.
Lisbon, ME 04250
(207) 650-7214
spunkyeclectic.com

TerraBellaSpun
terrabellaspun.etsy.com

bibliography

Casselman, Karen Diadick. *Lichen Dyes: The New Source Book*, second edition. Mineola, New York: Dover Publications Inc., 2001.

Grae, Ida. *Nature's Colors: Dyes from Plants*. McMinnville, Oregon: Robin & Russ Handweavers, 1974.

Feitelson, Ann. *The Art of Fair Isle Knitting: History, Technique, Color & Patterns*. Loveland, Colorado: Interweave, 1997.

Høxbro, Vivian. *Domino Knitting*. Loveland, Colorado: Interweave, 2002.

Isager, Marianne. *Classic Knits*. Loveland, Colorado: Interweave, 2009.

Menz, Deb. *Color in Spinning*. Loveland, Colorado: Interweave, 1998.

Roberts, Nancy. "Machine Knitting to Dye For." *Spin-Off*, 30, 3 (Fall 2006), 60–65.

Ross, Mabel. *The Essentials of Yarn Design for Handspinners*. Crook of Devon, Kinross, Scotland: M. Ross, 1983.

Royce, Beverly. *Notes on Double Knitting,* expanded edition. Pittsville, Wisconsin: Schoolhouse Press, 1994.

Schueler, Kristi. "Turning Batts into Roving." http://blog.designedlykristi.com/?p=465

Taylor, Kathleen. *Yarn to Dye For.* Loveland, Colorado: Interweave, 2005.

Thomas, Mary. *Mary Thomas's Book of Knitting Patterns*. Mineola, New York: Dover Publications Inc., 1972.

Walker, Barbara. *A Treasury of Knitting Patterns*. Pittsville, Wisconsin: Schoolhouse Press, 1998.

Waterman, Martha. *Traditional Knitted Lace Shawls*. Loveland, Colorado: Interweave, 1998.

Zawistoski, Patsy. "Navajo Plying Unraveled." *Spin-Off,* 15, 2 (Summer 1991), 86–88.

Zimmermann, Elizabeth. *Knitting Workshop*. Pittsville, Wisconsin: Schoolhouse Press, 1981.

contributor biographies

Kathryn Alexander is known for her colorful designs that feature innovative use of entrelac and her work with energized yarns to create dynamic knit surfaces. She lives on a small farm in upstate New York with her husband and two horses.

Sarah Anderson has always loved fiber. She is currently a dyer, knit designer, and all-around fiber enabler. She lives in Snohomish, Washington, with her husband, Dick, six spinning wheels, tons of wool, and an embarrassing number of spindles.

Jeannine Bakriges loves to spin, knit, dye for, and wear berets and tams. She makes her home in Whitingham, Vermont.

Nancy Bush owns The Wooly West, a mail-order yarn business in Salt Lake City, Utah. She is the author of *Knitted Lace of Estonia* (2008), *Knitting Vintage Socks* (2005), *Knitting on the Road: Socks for the Traveling Knitter* (2001), *Folk Knitting in Estonia* (1999), and *Folk Socks* (1994), all published by Interweave.

Kaye D. Collins of northern Colorado has been working with alpaca fiber since 1986. She teaches spinning and Andean knitting at conferences and retreats. She enjoys custom spinning and sells fine natural fibers from her studio/shop, Fiber to Fabric.

Emma Crew lives in the Pacific Northwest with her husband and two sons. When not immersed in family or fiber, she can be found singing with the Seattle Symphony Chorale.

Liz Gipson is the managing editor of *Handwoven* magazine, author of *Weaving Made Easy* (Interweave, 2008), co-host of *Knitting Daily TV*, and shepherdess to four precocious cashmere-bearing goats.

Erda Kappeler of Ukiah, California, learned to spin and weave in 1962, and her childhood love of fibers found an outlet. Over the years, she's met the nicest people through her fiber passions and reports that it has truly changed her life.

Amy King is the owner of the Spunky Eclectic webshop (spunkyeclectic.com) and bricks-and-mortar store in Maine. She is the author of *Spin Control* (Interweave, 2009).

Sara Lamb dyes, spins, weaves, and knits in her yurt studio in the foothills of northern California. She is the author of *Woven Treasures* (Interweave, 2009). Her work can be found at saralamb.com.

Faina Letoutchaia was born in St. Petersburg, Russia, where she started designing her own knitting garments in middle school. She began spinning recently when she was unable to find commercial lace yarns to her liking. Faina lives in East Lansing, Michigan.

Judith MacKenzie McCuin of Creston, Washington, has been a textile artist for over thirty years. She is the author of two books, most recently *The Intentional Spinner* (Interweave, 2008).

Amy Clarke Moore of Lakewood, Colorado, is the editor of *Spin-Off* magazine and the author of *Beaded Embellishment* (Interweave, 2002).

Diane Mulholland grew up on an Australian sheep farm, and a love of fiber was a natural result. Now living in London with her husband, she combines teaching and passion for fiber. Find her at dianemulholland.com.

Carol Huebscher Rhoades of Madison, Wisconsin, is *Spin-Off*'s technical editor and a frequent contributor to the magazine.

Nancy Roberts lives in the San Francisco Bay area. She is the owner of Machine Knitting to Dye For, where she teaches and sells equipment for machine knitting and dyeing self-striping yarns. Visit her website at machineknittingtodyefor.com.

Kristi R. Schueler spins, knits, designs, and teaches in Fort Collins, Colorado, where she resides with her husband and dog. Her work can be seen at blog.designedlykristi.com.

Lisa Shroyer is senior editor of *Interweave Knits* and editor of *Knitscene*. She comes from a fiber-loving family, having been taught to knit when she was eight years old by her mother, Nancy. Lisa has tried spinning, but it hasn't taken hold yet.

Nancy Shroyer is a knitter, spinner, dyer, weaver, teacher, and inventor. She owns Nancy's Knit Knacks with her husband, Bob.

Sarah Swett spins, knits, laughs, weaves tapestries, and drinks tea with friends in Moscow, Idaho. Sarah is the author of *Kids Weaving*.

Kathleen Taylor is the author of *Knit One, Felt Too; Yarns to Dye For* (Interweave, 2005); *I Heart Felt*; and *The Big Book of Socks*.

Kathryn Tewson knits, spins, writes, and sings—though not all at once! She lives in the suburbs of Seattle with her husband, Erik, and her two-year-old daughter, Lillian.

index

More Inspiring Books about Handspun Yarn

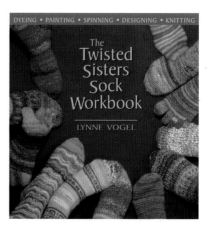